As I See It . . .
Views on International
Business Crises,
Innovations, and Freedom

As I See It . . . Views on International Business Crises, Innovations, and Freedom

The Impact on Our Daily Lives

Michael R. Czinkota

CETERUM CENSEO

BEP BUSINESS EXPERT PRESS

First published in 2017 by
Business Expert Press, LLC
222 East 46th Street, New York, NY 10017
www.businessexpertpress.com

ISBN-13: 978-1-63157-575-4 (paperback)
ISBN-13: 978-1-63157-576-1 (e-book)

Business Expert Press International Business Collection

Collection ISSN: 1948-2752 (print)
Collection ISSN: 1948-2760 (electronic)

Cover and interior design by S4Carlisle Publishing Services
Private Ltd., Chennai, India

First edition: 2017

10 9 8 7 6 5 4 3 2 1

Printed in the United States of America.

Dedication

To my wife Ilona and my daughter Margaret, the eyes of my life

Abstract

In this era of constant change and globalization, political and international issues influence the business environment worldwide and penetrate our lifestyle and expectations in ways beyond most imaginations. The increasing transparency of information provides easier access to current events, new concepts, and data. Yet we are bounded by the complexity of understanding the interdependence resulting from this fast-paced world with an almost overwhelming amount of new responsibilities. With a Foreword by H.E. Claudia Fritsche, Ambassador extraordinary and plenipotentiary, along with the humorous illustrations by award-winning cartoonist David Clark—*As I See It* . . . by Michael Czinkota is a fantastic choice for readers to comprehend the most crucial international business and trade issues facing us nowadays. Thought-provoking, witty, enjoyable, and providing new visions, this book offers fresh insights and perspectives which can inspire real-life understanding and applications one shall not miss.

Keywords

Crisis, Economy, Freedom, Globalization, Government, Innovation, International business, Marketing, Policy, Politics, Trade, Strategy

Contents

Foreword

H.E. Claudia Fritsche
Ambassador extraordinary and plenipotentiary
Washington D.C.
July 11, 2016

When I met Prof. Michael Czinkota in 2003, it had been less than 2 years since I had the privilege to establish the Liechtenstein Embassy in Washington. He immediately was very generous in offering to share his knowledge and experience. Since the field of economics is not my expertise, I was immensely grateful for his support in not only raising the profile of the Embassy but also helping me become acquainted with the many nuances and layers of the U.S. economy and its global impact. Since Prof. Czinkota was born and raised in Germany and was partly educated in an Austrian school very close to Liechtenstein, he is familiar with my country, with its history, its economic system as well as the trans-Atlantic cultural differences, therefore able to understand how the U.S. economy is viewed even from the perspective of a small country. Professor Czinkota further broadened his engagement with my country by teaching at the University of Liechtenstein.

Many visiting Liechtenstein dignitaries as well as LLM classes of the University of Liechtenstein have over the years had the opportunity to interact at Georgetown University's McDonough School of Business, upon invitation of Prof. Czinkota who offered a unique platform by including students and faculty in the subsequent discussions. Professor Czinkota, having had a distinguished career within the U.S. Administration, has a very special talent in reaching out to students as well as his colleagues to connect the academic world with private sector and Government representatives. He enabled Liechtenstein visitors to exchange views and learn more about what drives the U.S. economic system.

Being a leading researcher in the fields of international business and marketing, Prof. Czinkota is and continues to be a wealth of knowledge which he so wonderfully shares by writing concise pieces for key audiences, for business executives, and policy makers who cannot or will not put time aside to read elaborate manuscripts. I particularly like the combination of his findings with cartoons. A little humor never hurts, especially in combination with otherwise sometimes dry subjects. Jokes aside, this book is an important resource for experts and novices alike to gain an insightful perspective on the U.S. and global economies in a way that presents the numerous variables that impact our everyday lives in an easily comprehendible manner.

This book marks again Prof. Czinkota's distinct ability to blend different economic perspectives, those by the business sector, the policy makers and the academic world. The compilation of his articles and editorials reflect how business reaches even the most remote places on earth and how political developments have an immediate effect on the economy as such and international trade in particular.

I agree with Prof. Czinkota who says: "Reading this book will leave you with more understanding, smarter, and more capable of making this world better for all of us. Reading it for just three minutes before you fall asleep will make you the smartest person in the room the next day."

Introduction

Why You Should Read this Book. . .

This book presents "the best of 2016" about the core issues of international business, explained and analyzed within 750 words. It is hardly possible to read everything and be informed about what is happening in this world. This compilation of articles and editorials by Prof. Czinkota, which were published in news media worldwide, contains thoughtful insight into key dimensions of international business and trade. The vast array of themes—ranging from terrorism to business strategies in developing countries—reflect how international business reaches every corner of our world today. This volume makes much of this complexity more accessible by presenting the topics, its analysis and controversies, and possible new directions in a few pages—just enough for bed time reading so that when you wake up, you will be the smartest person in the room.

Only the first two articles introducing the sections are longer, since they set the stage for everything subsequent. Normally people expect medicine to taste bad. Insofar one might think of this first longer article; however, the article is fun to read and gives a general overview which will make you understand future issues.

Also, each analysis is accompanied by a cartoon, developed by Czinkota and award-winning cartoonist David Clark. Through the parsimonious use of the word and the frequent offer of insightful drawings, we hope to enhance understanding and appreciation of proverbial pictures and a thousand words on the international trade and investment environment.

We live in a global community in many ways; however, many sectors need to catch up to these approaches—such as international marketing and trade policies. In addition, an international market only functions through trust and relationships between merchants and companies. In spite of better communications across great distances, business relationships are still as important as ever, and will not be disappearing any time soon.

Political and international affairs directly impact every form of business. Just think the human condition on earth as a sphere where one slice is business, both affecting and being affected by other dimensions, be they medicine, religion, or thermodynamics. Readers are bombarded with a colossal volume of reports and articles, which can be overwhelming. Therefore, in spite of progress in transparency, it becomes increasingly burdensome to understand the effects of issues in a global market. This is why we offer these short commentaries, editorials, and cartoons to encourage comprehension of and thinking about the most important and relevant topics today without a total issue immersion for which most of us have too little time.

Most people fail to recognize what role they play in international trade. The vast majority of purchases made by consumers, from household goods to clothes to automobiles, incorporate parts that originate from different nations. This not only illustrates how integrated the global economy has become, but also shows how international trade leads to greater efficiency. As nations continue to export goods that they specialize in, the input cost for nearly every good and service imaginable declines. In addition, advances in shipping allow consumers to make international purchases online and have it sent directly to their home. This provides a broader array of options, leading to a more satisfied consumer who has money left over to pay for new or unexpected expenses, say, a boat which enriches life.

People enjoy the idea of free trade; however, many do not accept the consequences that come along. Internationalization denotes the ability to purchase satisfactory goods for a very low price. However, these goods will often come from other nations, which lead to a lower demand for the local industry output. This is a trade-off that comes with the reality of free trade. In addition, the role of the government has come into question in recent years, especially with regards to downturns in the economy. Some insist that government should intervene to help create jobs, while others argue that the government has already overstepped its boundaries in terms of everyday individual lives. The articles of this book touch on the natural ebb and flow in every economy and how set-backs actually bring about innovation and often inspire new business policies explained for increase efficiency. Recent recessions do not signal a decline on the world stage, but rather an opportunity to move forward with new determination and pursue different frontiers. At the same time, if we demand that government provides the greatest protection possible, then we have to be willing to give up a certain amount of privacy, as is discussed in the section about economic growth and freedom.

This book outlines some of the far-reaching consequences of international conflict and how marketing and trade can be tools to deal with these crises: From the refugee crisis, spy wars, to the ongoing conflict of between Russian and Ukraine, and global terrorism, all of these events cause people to divert investments elsewhere which raises the price of global trade. The second section of the book is dedicated to international innovations, such as strategies in developing countries and emerging concepts such as the Honorable Merchant. In its third part, the book elaborates how international marketing and trade play essential roles in strengthening freedom—in the United States and abroad. The last section shows the reader how the strong effects of international marketing and trade, from health care to the Super Bowl.

In closing, this book outlines important aspects of international business, and often does so with a bit of humor and in an entertaining manner. Do read this book, it will be fun, easy, and worthwhile. As a bonus, come to our blog MichaelCzinkota.com

Prof. Michael R. Czinkota

Georgetown University,   *University of Kent,*
Washington D.C., USA   *Canterbury, England*
czinkotm@georgetown.edu   *m.czinkota@kent.ac.uk*

January 1, 2017

Acknowledgments

The members of my research team who devoted large parts of their time and energy to the refinement and completion of this book and its chapters. In particular, I thank Maximilian Mareis, Shuo Zhang, Yang Yang, Lin Shi, Ayesha Malik, and all my business collaborators. Gratitude is also due to my Georgetown and Kent friends and colleagues, Professors Cooke, Ronkainen, Skuba, Meyer, and Gupta. Thank you Dean Lew Cramer and Martin Meyer for your strong support of the international cause. Chapeau to Deputy Dean Luc Wathieu for your support and for making the right comments at the right time. Your insights, efforts, and debates keep international business alive. I am also thankful to the kindness of the editors and newspapers who have given me permission to reprint my articles. Heartfelt thanks to David Clark, the award-winning artist who has provided the visual stimuli for this book and my annual calendar. Also thank you to my brother Thomas Czinkota, who often spends much of his weekend bouncing ideas and new directions between our minds which, more often than not, lead to new inspirations and perspectives. Thanks to his family Birgit, Michael, and Sarah for letting the two brothers have such a good time.

Most of all, I am grateful to my spouse Ilona Czinkota who is the major pundit helping the quality of my thinking and writing. Early or late in the day, she is always willing to provide ideas and suggestions. My daughter Margaret comments as well with much enthusiasm and verve. Our collaboration represents—I hope, high level early admissions training for Georgetown. Both mother and daughter are great sounding boards and arbiters, who come up with excellent questions and solutions.

Molto bene, grazie mille!

Michael R. Czinkota
Washington, D.C.
September 23, 2016

SECTION I

Dealing with Current Crises

CHAPTER 1

Securing America's International Business Future: An Overview (with P. Dickson)

Marketing News, April 2016

Not many annual reports highlight the surprise of success.

This first article is longer than the subsequent articles; however, it is still fun to read and, more importantly, guarantees a general overview which will make you understand crucial changes in international trade and marketing.

Twenty years ago, we presented a process-learning perspective on what was needed to ensure that America continues to be a winner in free trade markets and a shining city on the hill. Drawing on how Great Britain lost its lead in the industrial revolution, we proposed several integrated programs to promote the process-learning market. Central to this was the creation of well-paying jobs through superior commercialization of innovation.

Since then, individuals such as Michael Porter have been outspoken about the need for a major public policy-driven innovation initiative, but little action has resulted. Interest in the topics of learning and innovation has actually declined in public discourse over the past 11 years as measured by *Google Trends* in Figure 1.1. It should have increased instead.

Meanwhile the world has moved on. The extraordinary growth of Asian economies, in particular China's over the past 20 years has dramatically altered the challenges and raised the stakes. According to the World Bank, in terms of port container traffic, the Chinese economy has grown logistically from being about equal to the United States in 2000 to being four times larger in 2015, as shown in Figure 1.2.

Judging by these traffic flows, a lot more experiential learning is being done in the Chinese economy and it is not just learning how to move containers. It is learning how to develop, market, and distribute new products to the market. Learning-by-doing has made many sectors of the Chinese economy more capable and competitive than their counterparts in the United States. This enormous learning advantage gained by active international traders, many of them from Asia, appears to have been insufficiently recognized by the political and business leadership of the United States. Failure to learn because of not doing will lead to diminished results for

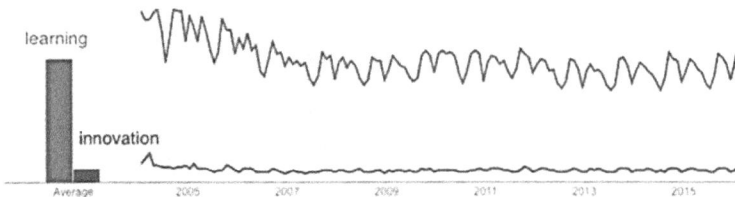

Figure 1.1 Frequency of learning and innovation

Source: Google Trends (www.google.com/trends), from 2005 to 2015

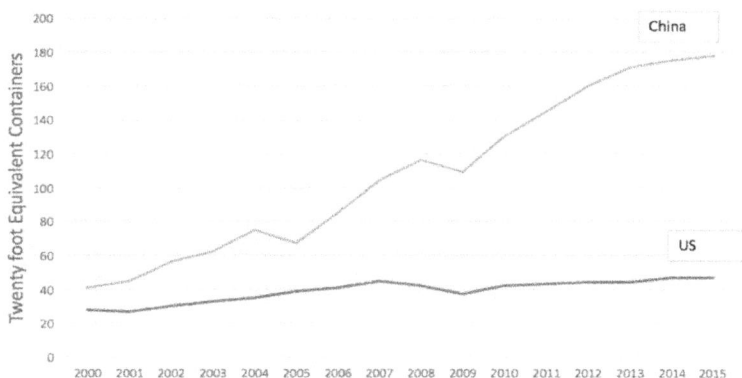

Figure 1.2 China and U.S. container traffic, 2000–2015

Source: World Bank World Development Indicators (WDIs), Economic Commission for Latin America and the Caribbean (ECLAC) and China Port Container official website, February 2015.

the U.S. economy. It will bring lower wages and greater income inequality to the United States over the next several decades. We propose a number of public–private sector initiatives that can be implemented rapidly by a new administration to rebuild the nation's competence and confidence in its process-learning capabilities and commercialization of innovation. But first the story behind why these initiatives are needed.

How the Business World Has Changed

Much pivots from innovations in transportation, communication, and logistics. The key trade barrier that reduced competition between national economic enterprises was the prohibitive cost of transporting products safely to faraway destinations. The impact of this trade barrier has shifted due to lower tariffs, and better information flows. Declining energy prices contribute to low transportation costs. Innovation has led to higher trade volume. Research has found a positive and statistically significant correlation between innovation and export. Manufacturing and distribution quality control were supported by the innovation of at-a-distance systems controls, such as ISO9000 certification and performance contracts.

As collateral effects, these breakthroughs have accelerated the learning of foreign suppliers, and created cheap and seamless logistic flows between low labor cost (LLC) economies and Western markets. Marketplace technology transfers between developed and developing economies now occur at a breakneck speed. Online tools are the new reality that permit the legal transfer of ideas from innovator to imitator at almost no cost and in real time. Beyond that, the Internet has empowered the theft of intellectual property estimated to cost U.S. companies more than $300 billion per year.

American business ideas support America's competitors. American higher education transfers its newest thoughts and practices to the world's knowledge workers as a deliberate business development strategy. American multinational company managers increase owner profits by transferring ideas and value-added processes to their global supply chains and operations in LLC economies. Sadly, the transfer prices typically charged are based on the cost of knowledge replication rather than that of knowledge regeneration, thus providing very little recovery of investment capital.

The Learning Curve Advantage of Imitators

Transfers to offshore imitators reinforce those who already possess a steeper learning curve than the original innovator. An imitator's learning curve is always steeper than the original innovator's learning curve. However fast we move into new fields, the rest of the world will catch up faster. As illustrated in Figure 1.3's learning curve, in many technologies, U.S. businesses are at the top, whereas Chinese businesses are half-way up and thus learning faster and more.

Also, American firms often follow traditional and conservative improvement methods. Many Asian companies in contrast find innovative ways of dealing with new issues, letting them climb even faster.

The advantage, however, flips when American innovation frequency creates new firms, markets, and learning curves. Then, American companies are on the steep part of the learning S curve whereas Chinese and many other Asian start-ups are still at the fermenting stage. One interesting observation here is that younger firms have more to gain than older firms from increasing sales through exports. Sadly, however, U.S. intensity of start-up activity of firms is declining or tepid at best. In some quarters, there is expectation of a growing firm founders' gap, which causes the United States to fall behind.

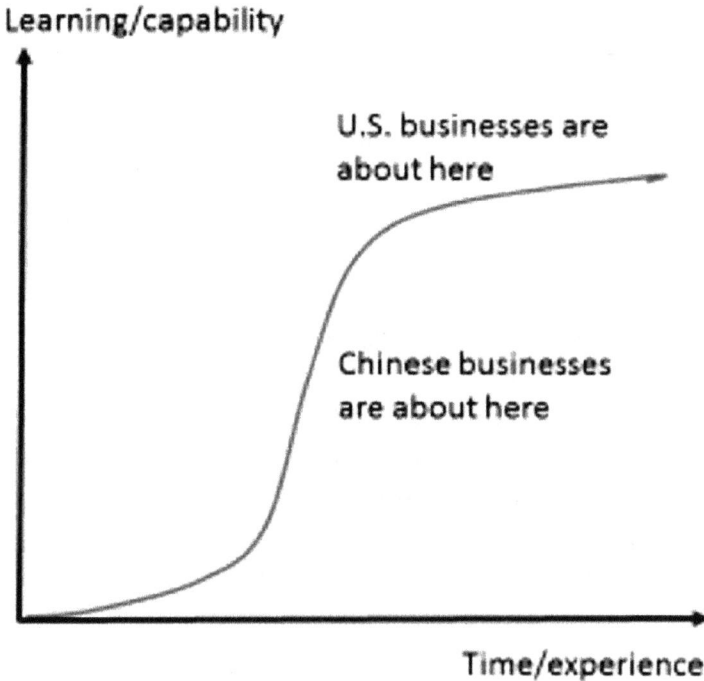

Figure 1.3 Business positions on the learning curve

Strategic constraints can, if understood well, also help the success of the underdog. We have established the benefits which Asian imitators can obtain from American innovators. There is, however, no prohibition of an imitation strategy by U.S. firms. We already do so with Indian products and services, such as the radio (1895 in Calcutta) and the discovery of water on the lunar surface (2013), and Chinese products for the Fourth of July fireworks (7th century AD), or, in future, with the Beijing Electron Positron Collider (BEPC) (2016). Any firm or industry that can position itself on the steep part of the "S" curve through imitation can have an advantage above the Overlord. The bottom line: Imitation strategies can work for American firms too!

Experience Curves and Exports

In studying the effect of experience, the Boston Consulting Group (BCG 2016) found costs on value added to go down 20 to 30 percent every time cumulative output doubles. BCG attributes this decline to greater managerial, production, and logistical expertise arising from greater product experience, leading to lower costs. Small firms can rapidly decrease their high initial costs, since their cumulative volume tends to be small and can be doubled and redoubled quickly. Thus, a good way for a new firm to compete with an established one is to increase sales volume rapidly, thus quickly lowering its costs, even if this strategy hurts short-term profits.

Exporting can be a key strategy for new and young firms to do so. By selling outside the domestic market to more customers, small firms gain more rapidly in product experience and decrease unit costs, and are better able to compete with established larger firms. Larger firms, on the other hand, do not have as much to gain by increasing their sales volume through exporting, as they have already obtained earlier significant cumulative outputs in the domestic market.

The Enterprise Development Dynamic

The effects of logistics innovation, accelerated technology transfer, and learning advantage loomed large in the 1980s when American supply chain capabilities leapt forward. The actual cost of distribution as a percentage of GDP declined while the quality of service went up. Distribution bundlers such as FedEx flourished. Many companies rerouted their supply chains through LLC economies to stay price competitive and increase their profits. Otherwise, they were outcompeted and investment dried up.

This shift is not unexpected according to Vernon and Wells, whose product cycle theory concludes that profitable innovations require large quantities of capital and highly skilled labor. Innovating countries increase their exports while competitors exercise downward pressure on prices and profit margins.

For mature products, manufacturing is completely standardized. The availability of cheap and unskilled labor dictates the country of production. Profit margins are thin, and competition is fierce. Exports peak as the LLC countries expand production and become net exporters themselves.

Initiation of production in the United States and the moving of factories abroad can well be done by the same firm. Transfer of production locale may mean a job loss for employees but is not necessarily a loss of competitiveness for the firm. Yet, without any planning for transition, the value of unemployed workers quickly races toward zero. This is unacceptable and explains why re-shoring must become a new preference. Currently, the dynamic progresses through these steps:

1. Western engineers and managers set up production lines that meet desired quality standards in LLC economies. Western technology and manufacturing innovation that fit with the LLC worker skills, work ethic, and costs are transferred to new supply chain partners.
2. With increasing manufacturing experience, both costs and quality defects go down (the experience curve). Supply chain partners innovate processes that increase quality and reduce costs continuously.
3. Goods supplied by supply chain partners start to be sold in the LLC domestic economy at low prices, encouraging local markets and brand growth. Source nations such as China, India, Indonesia, Mexico, and Brazil create new powerful brands that are world class.
4. The new brands are marketed and sold in other emerging markets where they often outcompete established Western brands.
5. The new brands absorb share and profitability in Western economies.
6. New brands become of higher quality and outcompete established brands.

The above development dynamic expands around the globe. Highly motivated, education-focused workers and companies will likely design and deliver better lean products and services to global markets than those less motivated, interested, and educated.

Reality creates not just a labor market problem but also a capital market problem. Investment may continue to flow through and greatly enrich Wall Street, but it will pool where the action is—which is Main Road, PRC, where markets, jobs, and capital are created.

New patterns of trade have, often seamlessly, integrated U.S. interests even without effective industrial policy. Localized competitiveness used to encourage innovation. The United States' economy remains large, variable and vibrant, and its consumers are loyal to domestic products. In consequence any decline tends to be gradual without a view of the abyss. But the slow, intermittent nature makes the situation highly insidious. Like the slowly cooked frog, who does not notice the rising heat, there is no alarm to trigger broad-based sacrifices in support of decisive action.

Being Great at Certain Things

Here are some possible remedies.

1. Rapidly increase the number and proportion of new firms.
2. Encourage and assist with the cost of training process improvement expertise. Highlight innovations that have systemwide effects.
3. Sponsor research and training centers focused on supporting new processes, such as big data analysis through cross-collaboration for example, between the Commerce Department, the SBA, the International Trade Commission, and AID.
4. Have public and private sectors jointly create pop-up research centers that better train process improvers, and domestically distribute insights of companies that innovate successfully.
5. The Commerce Department should assert its communication role by patronizing an annual case competition with key examples of how international business obstacles have been creatively overcome through process innovation.
6. The U.S. Commercial Service should identify key global innovators, from whom it can acquire process information and distribute such as a clearing house or seminar coordinator both for American innovators and imitators. Government servants had to learn for more than a decade that service exports are just as good as exports from manufacturing plants. Now, they must learn to appreciate American imitation and support it as an information-clearing house, and perhaps even through export fireside chats. While we strongly support the gathering and distribution of targeted information focused on interested firms, we do not support the selection of winners and losers.
7. There is a need for an ongoing thrust in support of innovation—maybe through an Innovators' Day, when firms can brag a little

and crown their key contributors to innovation. There could even be innovation competitions in schools, reminiscent of spelling bees, and an annual School District innovation runoff.

There is nothing demeaning about supporting business which has made America great! Government, firms, and employees need to write a new history. Training and support of knowledge workers who help to commercialize *American* innovation, imitation, and incubation is crucial. It is imperative to periodically evaluate how support and funding for international business programs translate into success. The goal is to increase American knowledge workers' likelihood of producing innovative goods that outsell global competition, allow America's economy to adapt and move into newer fields quicker and more successfully than anyone else, and ensure that the American economy profits from freer trade.

Innovation Scholarships can be awarded to local students and faculty with the best commercializing innovation ideas for the three business sectors most important to each state's economy. Of crucial importance is to not let such awards become captive to one interest group. Rather, there must be an early cross-fertilization between fields, for example venture capitalists, successful academics, service experts, and engineers. University business incubators have been successful in cultivating exactly such an environment. The Halcyon Incubator floated by the S&R Foundation is just one example of this success. The sponsorship of a meaningful number of scholarships would consume only a fraction of the savings achieved by forthcoming U.S. base closures in Europe.

Each team will nurture a start-up business venture around the central innovator's idea. Higher education should be expected, using its own endowment funds, to invest in a portfolio of job-creating business ventures. These should be limited to 2 years for any given project and end with a major attempt to secure crowd funding. Concurrently, a series of innovation and imitation presentations, starting at the local level and continuing upwards, can enlighten and encourage supporters and participants. Such collaboration between fields and facility has already been applied quite successfully in Germany.

Figure 1.4 indicates the necessity for and a benchmark of some key terms: trade deficit, export promotion, and competitiveness. They reflect

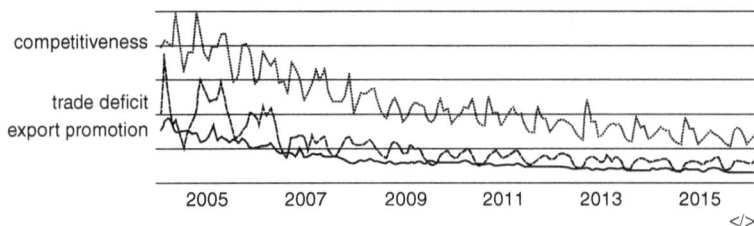

Figure 1.4 **Frequency-of-mention: trade deficit, competitiveness, and export promotion**

competitiveness: dotted line; trade deficit: dashed line; export promotion: solid line

Source: Google Trends (www.google.com/trends), from 2005 to 2015, e.g. Google Trends (www .google.com/trends) on Trade deficit, competitiveness, export promotion, from 2005 to 2015.

the positioning for the U.S.' international business policy actions and outlook. While the apparent loose correlation between the three factors in general appeals for a partial linkage between them, we find the downslide, which occurred for all three factors during the past 11 years, to be quite troublesome.

In summary, we recommend a sustained decade-long deployment of government and higher education resources to provide incentives that encourage planning and training for the facilitation of creating additional, younger and more internationally oriented firms. The firms then must be provided with dedicated workers and a supportive broad-based educational infrastructure, and successful management capable and willing to innovate, imitate, and internationalize. The youth of this nation must again think of progress in terms of internationally commercializing its work. After all, they are the future!

CHAPTER 2

The Cost of Terrorism Keeps on Rising

Korea Times, December 2015

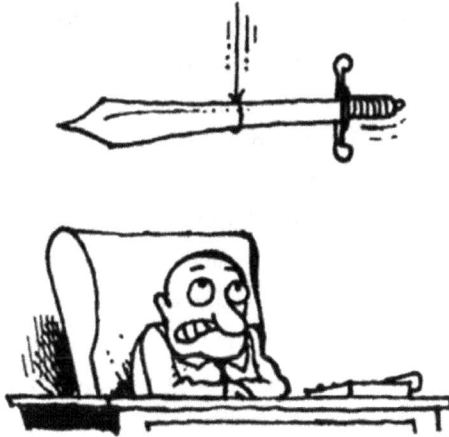

The sword of Damocles – early portent of
today's CEO.

The recent attacks in Paris by the Islamic State (ISIS) have again turned the spotlight onto terrorism. The IS, which emerged from Iraq and has taken over large portions of Iraq and Syria, is also threatening Europe and other regions. The invocation of terrorism has never gone away regionally, with almost daily reports of killings, bombs, and suicide missions. But now terrorism has become ubiquitous, and reaches nations which typically resolve conflicts through peaceful means. Since 2001, apart from many local killings, there have been separate large-scale attacks on the

United Kingdom, Spain, India, and Russia. Where we used to differentiate our analysis from a philosophical, existential, and economic perspective between the "civilized" and the "uncivilized" world, we now have to
cast our vote between barbarous and nonbarbarous adversaries.

One major impact of terrorism will be on travel and tourism. *The
New York Times* recently reported that current numbers of tourists are already
showing a slight decrease to areas that have experienced terrorist attacks. This
is especially significant for France, which had 84 million foreign visitors last
year and for which travel and tourism accounts for nearly 9 percent of its
economy. Flight cancellations to Paris were felt days after the attack. Bookings
for future trips have dropped by a third as compared to last year's numbers. A
similar situation occurred in the United States after the September 11, 2001,
attacks and according to statistics from the United States Office for Travel and
Tourism, it took 5 years for international visits to exceed their 9/11 numbers.

Tight security regulations and very strict border control are some
of the factors that contributed to the decrease in foreign visits. Europe,
which relies heavily on tourism, may be adversely affected by the recent
Paris attacks if movement across the 26 countries in the Schengen region
will be restricted. Already, we are seeing temporary border controls being
erected in light of the migration crisis in the Middle East and Africa.
Once in place, new security measures might be hard to dismantle again.

With the Euro zone experiencing the slowest growth in years, the Paris
attacks may do great harm to the already weak economies in the region.
Last month, *Forbes* reported that spending during the busiest business
month of the year may be curbed. The transfer of goods across boundaries
could greatly affect the manufacturing industries in the region. And with
businesses poised to expand to countries in the Middle East, the recent
attacks may halt those plans.

Another outcome of the terrorism threat has been a rise of public–
private partnerships, in which governments and firms collaborate to
counter terrorism. For example, global police agencies now partner
regularly with private firms to combat cyber-crime and attacks on critical
computer infrastructure. Governments and activist groups now use social
media to organize campaigns fighting against threats ranging from dictators to disease. But nations also have begun to curtail social media when
they are contrary to government interests.

Policy measures intended to increase security may lessen the efficiency of global transportation and logistical systems. The unintended consequences of such actions may increase market imperfections and raise business costs further, and may alter the environment in many ways more harmful to business interests than the terrorist events that provoked them. While everyone can agree on the need to guard against terrorism, a key question is always: Who pays?

From a global perspective, terrorism's effects are present for many firms, even those who see themselves as quite remote from any location affected by terrorism. Today's climate of global commerce involves extensive interaction with countless distributors and customers. Producers and marketers rely on suppliers and suppliers' suppliers to obtain goods and components. Such extensive networks increase the exposure of firms to events that take place at a far distance. Even firms perceived as having little international involvement may depend on the receipt of imported goods and are therefore subject to shortages or delays of inputs and the disruption of company operations.

An article by Professor Sheffi of MIT cites the importance of having to understand that in today's business climate of global competition and rapid response, firms no longer have the luxury of just aiming for "survival" in case of a terror attack. Instead, firms need to be flexible in order to be able to withstand shocks. They must offer assured continuity to their suppliers, their clients, their employees, and other stakeholders in order to inspire confidence in the relationship. Flexible firms will recover more quickly and can more readily sustain performance in the aftermath of terrorism's direct and indirect consequences. Firms need to develop continuity plans to deal with crises. Such plans may, for example, facilitate a shift of production to different regions of the world in the wake of unanticipated disruptive events. Particularly for firms that engage in massive outsourcing, the reliance on a single or even limited number or locations of suppliers, is quite risky. Ongoing business relationships after a terrorist incident need to be a principal goal of any firm. Apart from the importance of such an achievement for the viability of the firm, business continuity also denies terrorists their achievements.

Especially small- and medium-sized enterprises have limited resources and competing priorities. Managers are disinclined to plan for contingencies that (a) may occur at some distant future time (e.g., not this quarter), (b) involve high levels of uncertainty and are therefore difficult to measure and plan for, and (c) shareholders and stakeholders view as relatively unimportant. A key challenge for policy makers, therefore, is to stimulate managers to invest the time and money to deal with the threat and possible effects of terrorism and other emergencies.

CHAPTER 3

The U.S. Senate Report on Torture: Curative International Marketing as a Remedy (with Thomas Czinkota)

OVI Magazine, December 2014

Protecting one target well may only make
others more vulnerable.

The U.S. Senate report on the treatment of Islamic extremist captives has dealt a major blow to the reputation of American exceptionalism. "Curative International Marketing" (CIM) can help restore the brand equity loss of the United States.

The report recounts the torture employed, with interrogation results which were insubstantial in the war against terrorism. Directly and indirectly, the use of repellant interrogation techniques has soiled Americans with terrorist muck. The use of intermediaries or a stump in the chain of command do not provide plausible deniability. "Stomach slaps" and "rectal rehydration" gnaw on the tree of freedom. But remorse alone is insufficient.

At Georgetown University's McDonough School of Business, we have worked for several years on the concept of CIM as a new direction for countries and businesses, very apropos to the current ingloriousness. We use the term "curative" to connote restoration and development of international societal health. "Restoring" indicates something lost which once was there. "Development" refers to new issues, new tools, and new frames of reference. "Health" clarifies the importance to overall welfare, all of which marketing can address and improve. "International" carries the concept across borders.

Some may be distracted by the term "marketing." Yet one needs to consider that any complaints, accusations, and malfeasances will, in the first place, affect businesses in their public efforts around the globe. Firms will be shunned, deserted, and even attacked. It is their marketing efforts which will dissipate hatred. Also, when troops, interrogations, and drones become insufficiently effective, business activities are the action sector which can most quickly and clearly communicate and display high morals. Particularly with focused education and training, managers can emphasize that not all that can be done, should be done. Since firms know that they will be the first to pay the price of hatred abroad, they also need to be the ones to dedicate themselves most rapidly to the restoration of a reputation symmetry.

CIM takes responsibility for problems which a society and its members have generated. Marketing can help set morally wrong actions right and rebuild the wellbeing of individuals and society globally. Curative marketing determines what wrong has been wrought and then initiates future action to make up for past errors.

Moving on is not enough! Mistakes inflicted on society cannot be swept under the carpet. Errors fester like a destructive virus culture. One needs the spirit of "Wiedergutmachung" or restitution. A curative marketing approach is instrumental for governments, managers, and firms in their work on the pylons crucial for a firm position of the shining city on the hill: Truthfulness, simplicity, less pressure, more participation, and personal responsibility.

Truthfulness: Citizens have either been actively mislead, or been left with a sense of substantial ambiguity. Curative actions must be based on fact and insight rather than emotions within the context of societal change. One must restore a presumptive burden of honesty.

Simplicity: Simplicity adds value and is crucially linked to truthfulness, learning, and making sure that one knows and understands the implications of decisions. More knowledge and training make it easier to be truthful.

Less pressure: To soar is only one mode of behavior, even for eagles. Sometimes there is too much effort aimed to expand too fast. It may be time for a slow food era.

More participation: A new international outlook must make allowances for others. Inclusiveness helps with future change when power waxes and wanes. One tendency is to focus on and celebrate winners. But when the rising tide arrives, leaking hulls, untrained crews, and porous sails will only lead to major discontent.

Personal responsibility: Distance does not remove responsibility. One can no longer use intermediaries and, later on, be suitably astonished, surprised, and mortified about their actions. Realistically, locals take even distant actions quite personally. Although there is frequent talk about mutual understanding, the actual overlap between societies remains miniscule. The average Chinese person understands as much about Columbus, Ohio, as the average American does about Tianjin, China.

Governments again assert a growing role. New global regulations and restrictions are not always free from fault and ambition. Global discord is growing. Conflict is not resolved by simply moving on. One needs to invest the time and effort to systematically rebuild the trust and admiration to which the United States used to be accustomed. The sad conditions are a clarion call for CIM. Nobody is perfect, but a fair compensatory effort can restore many opportunities. A strong international and moral presence by the U.S. and its businesses can well be a carrier and agent of positive change. At the frontline, they can mend the broken dreams and fears of America.

CHAPTER 4

Anti-Corruption War: Western Ways Doomed to Fail (with Anna Astvatsatryan)

Sri Lanka Guardian, December 2014

Laughing when others trip is called
"Schadenfreude", and not just in Germany.

In November of this year, leaders of the Group of Twenty (G20) vowed to implement an anti-corruption action plan. Although the proposed strategies might improve the situation for G20 member states, using the same toolkit will not work in the developing world. One needs to take into account culture, traditions, and historical circumstances, when crafting anti-corruption strategies for the developing world.

It has been more than a quarter century that industrialized countries began their anti-corruption crusade. International organizations and developed economies offer a standard toolkit of programs to fight corruption such as changing education systems, enforcing legislation against domestic and foreign bribery, increasing transparency of the government, and combating money laundering. Every year, Transparency International produces the corruption perception index (CPI). A one-generation effort has been dedicated to the reduction of corruption and bribery, but, unfortunately, has not led to major changes. Countries where bribes and corruption are not perceived as corruption have not shifted their positions in the rankings. Where giving a bribe to an official was wrong 25 years ago, people still perceive bribery as a routine transaction. The top ten corrupt countries remain the same. These findings were based on the Global Corruption Barometer—a Transparency International survey that includes 114,000 people in 107 countries.

It is important to understand that countries with high levels of corruption are more likely to be governed by corrupt officials. Many established businesses are either owned by government officials or their family members, or have other personal connections to the government. According to a study at University of Texas, corrupt connections can negatively affect export capacity of a country. Major government-connected companies in transitional economies, are less likely to export, as they get more preferential treatment and artificial competitive advantage at home. In addition, these companies are used to the business practices specific to their home market and know all other major players. These biased conditions make them less competitive in the international trade, which therefore reduces the volume of exports. High-level government corruption will also affect the outcomes of the majority of international projects in cooperation with local governments. When in early 2000s, the Turkish Parliament investigated allegations of corruption of its two former prime ministers, it looked like the beginning of a serious anti-corruption campaign. However, soon a decision of the Parliament cleared them of charges. This news raised eyebrows in the global community.

Some countries are not ready to participate in wide ranging anti-corruption actions and prefer to act on their own. China's latest anti-corruption campaign has been criticized for being more of a weak attempt rather than structured anti-corruption effort. The arrests of key members of the Communist Party have so far not been followed by deeper investigation. In addition, China raised a last-minute objection to the G20 anti-corruption plan by refusing to support the principles of transparency that would help fight against shell companies engaged in tax evasion and money laundering. In fact, in 2014, China ranked 100th according to Transparency International, dropping 20 places from last year. In systems, where corruption is firmly established, it is oftentimes dangerous to be the whistleblower. For example, in the Czech Republic, 95% of citizens believe that corruption is prevalent at all levels of the government. However, there are no whistleblower protection laws, so many people are actually afraid of being persecuted for exposing cases of high-level corruption.

Culture and history can also represent big obstacles for fighting corruption. In India and Hungary, it is widely accepted to bribe a doctor or an official in order to skip the line and get better service. According to a study at the KOF Swiss Economic Institute in Zurich, in heavily regulated and burdensome entry markets, entrepreneurs often use bribes to facilitate the start of operations. Bribes are considered a greasing mechanism that helps accelerate business processes rather than do harm. De Jong and Bogmans of the University of Amsterdam found that in some countries, bribes are triggering imports, as they allow companies to bypass the waiting times and paperwork at customs. A study by Fisman and Miguel has found that diplomats from corrupt countries are usually getting more parking tickets, but are less likely to pay them. This is another illustration of how deeply rooted a cultural and historical mindset can be, and how it can manifest itself abroad.

Industrialized countries are still struggling with corruption and bribery within. In 2013, multiple organ transplant centers across Germany were placed under criminal investigation over allegations of waiting list manipulation. These revelations of bribery and dishonesty staggered public trust toward the health care system. Can developed countries defeat corruption worldwide, when they still have very serious bribery cases domestically. When crafting strategies to defeat corruption both in developing countries and domestically, leading economies should focus more on culture, traditions, and historical circumstances of each country. Building trusting relationships between the businesses and individuals will create internal capacities to fight corruption, and develop understanding of the negative effects of corruption within developing economies.

CHAPTER 5

The Volkswagen Crisis: A Lesson in Trust

Japan Today, September 2015

It's hard to get to the top and so easy to fall.

The Volkswagen crisis, triggered by misleading emission measurements, has reinforced the idea that truthfulness and simplicity are pillars of international marketing and integral to a business' public face. The (formerly) largest car manufacturer in terms of sales has been accused of fitting defeat devices into its diesel cars in the United States that can discern when the vehicle is undergoing emissions testing and turn on full emissions control for that duration. Once the testing is over, however, the emission controls are switched off and allow the cars to emit between

10 and 40 times the regulation standard of nitrogen oxide. Since this deception has come to light, Volkswagen's stocks have crashed, with shares falling 38 percent in 2 days. This initial loss to investors and the brand alike showcases the importance of truthfulness in business operations.

Businesses are constrained by the nations and societies in which they operate. Their standards of conduct should ensure that their business activities are beneficial to the people and society. Companies that are seen to violate such expectations will see their trustworthiness diminished. Reduced trust not only results in tangible losses for the company in terms of fines and costs of recall, but also causes the public to censure the company via strongly diminished sales. In order to regain the trust of the consumers, Volkswagen must engage with both short- and long-term measures.

Already, Volkswagen takes important steps to punish those responsible (either directly or via neglect) for the violation of the emission standards and the disappointment of the public's trust. Within 5 days, CEO Martin Winterkorn has resigned although he denies having any knowledge of the wrongdoing. The pressure of stakeholders, who lost trust in his leadership and were pushing him to leave was simply too high. What power does a CEO still hold, if the majority of shareholders are losing trust? Additional heads will roll with lay-offs signaling to the public that the company expects adherence to high standards of behavior, and is not lenient on those that break the social contract. Volkswagen has also set aside 6.5 billion euros ($7.3 billion) to cover the costs of recalling the cars with the defeat device, as well as any other damages. The U.S. Environmental Protection Agency (EPA) was given the power to fine a corporation up to $37,500 for each car that breaches standards—in Volkswagen's case that will result in a maximum fine of about $18 billion. Although the American government holds the harshest measures of all public sector actors, the private legal actions by car owners and shareholders of Volkswagen are not even considered and their claim "cannot be estimated at the current time" as VW said.

Together with future direct and indirect costs, this step curtails the company's profits for years to come. Yet it goes a long way in indicating that Volkswagen is ready to accept responsibility and do what it must in reparation of the betrayal of the trust which customers and governments had placed in the company. Public trust is an important determinant of a society's willingness to allow international firms to do business in their nations. Volkswagen will have to rebuild this broken trust, and reinforce the values of truthfulness and simplicity in its workings. No longer will VW consumers allow the company's real activities to be shrouded in complexity, or permit the lines of truthfulness to be blurred. For Volkswagen, standards will be scrutinized more and enforced more sharply. The European Commission already announced to revise the European standards and to introduce new testing technologies, which is more representative of on-road conditions.

Volkswagen ways of doing business must become more transparent and understandable by the public. For a company that is at the heart of Germany's manufacturing and export economy, and thought to reflect the social responsibility and consciousness of its home country, this active misleading of regulations and claims is a shock for supporters, customers, fellow firms, and host cities. Volkswagen will have to prove itself anew as an honest partner, an uphill task considering the magnitude of the deception and the corresponding stain on the car manufacturer's reputation which has "People's Car" as its name.

CHAPTER 6

Of Crimea and Punishment

Armenian News, August 2014

In battle, plans may not work but they do
shorten response time.

The conflicts between Russia and Ukraine have pitted Western countries against Russia. Some Russian officials no longer can travel abroad, and international investment and trade are restricted. Russian President Vladimir Putin, in turn, plans retaliatory sanctions against the United States and Western Europe by restricting Russian food imports and energy exports. Governments attempt to impose comparable sanction burdens on each other. However, due to cultural and historic differences, a policy based mainly on sanctions will lead to inequities and therefore substantially increase the risk in international trade.

Key differences exist between Russia and Western nations regarding profit, competition, risk and reward, private property and growth, and how they affect the outcome of sanctions. In the U.S., profit is the expected result of doing business and low profits are usually blamed on management. By contrast, lower profits in Russia allow its government to shift the blame onto foreign culprits.

Private property is a key reward in the U.S., whereas in Russia "private" often means responsibility and risk exposure. Since growth is key in the U.S., any inhibitors of growth are seen with concern. A wide variety of economic performance in Russia makes its growth much less of a pressure point. Sanctions against the U.S. may burden the population and lead to new candidates and policies. In Russia, the sacrifices imposed by sanctions seem to indicate dedication and strength. Declining U.S. profits or growth cause doomsday scenarios, while time is expected to bring economic improvement.

Losing out on the very latest technology means falling behind for Americans. For Russians, pretty good technology is a pretty good achievement. Russian ownership of space ferries and satellites and their use by the U.S. makes them proud.

Russia's size of 6.6 million square miles makes it geographically the largest country in the world. The 324 million U.S. population more than doubles that of Russia. Still, the Russian market is of great importance for many global firms. Moreover, Russia is a crucial player for other countries as a vital trading partner and a worldwide leader in the production of hydrocarbons. Russia was the second largest producers and exporter of crude oil after Saudi Arabia in 2015. Russia is the world's biggest gas exporter and many countries, especially in the European Union, depend highly on Russian exports of both. All the countries in Eastern Europe, with the exception of Poland, receive over 80 percent of their gas imports from Russia. Even if the Russian leadership is not touching their energy exports, Europe will feel under-heightened pressure if the spiral of sanctions is not stopped.

Although the European Union's sanctions were deliberately crafted to hit the Russian leadership and not the common Russian citizen, the increasing spiral of sanctions are hitting hard the Russian general economy and the ordinary citizens. There are only few historical rewards for former leaders. For example, although Greece invented the Olympic Games, no points are given for that ancient super action. Going first with the Greek flag when marching into the Olympic Stadium is just about all there is. Russia may well see its existing strength and market size as an opportunity for leadership.

We all are said to understand each other so much better than in the past. Yet, much of our thinking is based on our history, culture, and outlook. They define our spheres of interest which we aim to preserve. Ukraine, for example, will tend to be closer to Russia than to the United States. While before the crisis, Ukraine was split in two parts, the crises changed that. Now Russia garners negative ratings from Ukrainians in both the west (81 percent unfavorable) and the east (61 percent) of the country.

Culture is also influencing how countries perceive each other. For Russia, the end of the Cold War and the dissolution of the Soviet Empire is seen as a catastrophe—in stark contrast to the American perception as a glorious and merry revolution. The average Russian understands as much about Columbus, Ohio as the average American does about Sevastopol.

Global relationships between Russia, Asia, Europe, and the United States are being rebalanced. Key changes are likely to come from outside the United States. It would be unwise to undertake transformations without dampening the key concerns of key players on all sides.

CHAPTER 7

Terrorism and International Business (with Gary Knight and Gabriele Suder)

Japan Today, September 2011

**Crisis plans: plans for a crisis or
a crisis for plans?**

The airplanes of 9/11 forced countless multinational corporations (MNCs) to update their strategic planning. Our work with executives of more than 150 MNCs shows that 10 years later, companies are still grappling with how best to manage the terrorist threat.

In the two decades before 2001, the rate at which firms launched international ventures was growing rapidly. After 9/11, foreign direct investment fell dramatically as firms withdrew to their home markets.

The popularity of international-sounding company and brand names decreased appreciably as managers now emphasize domestic and local affiliations.

The tendency to reverse course on globalization has been accompanied by declining international education in the United States, as revealed by falling enrollments in foreign language and international business courses. In the past decade, managers shifted much of their focus from proactive exploration of international opportunities to a defensive posture emphasizing threats and vulnerable foreign operations. In Europe, the radicalization of individuals and groups, motivated by ideology, religion or economic concerns, threatens local cooperation and social harmony. European business schools have benefited from tighter restrictions on international student enrolments in the United States, but the focus of teaching has shifted from global to regional trade.

Another outcome of the terrorism threat has been a rise of public–private partnerships, in which governments and firms collaborate to counter them. For example, global police agencies now partner regularly with private firms to combat cyber-crime and attacks on critical computer infrastructure. Governments and activist groups now use social media to organize campaigns fighting against threats ranging from dictators to disease. But nations also have begun to curtail social media when they are contrary to government interests.

The cost of protecting against terrorism is high with billions of dollars, while terrorist spend millions or less on their actions. There are abundant opportunities for small groups to employ no-weapon technologies, such as aircraft, to cause massive harm. Although our capacity to protect key facilities has improved over time, the security focus on high-value assets encourages terrorists to redirect their violence at "soft targets" such as transportation systems and business facilities. Greater security at home means attacks will increasingly take aim on firms' foreign operations.

Companies have placed more emphasis on terrorism risk considerations when choosing how to enter foreign markets. In the last century, foreign direct investment (FDI) was the preferred approach. But terrorism has shifted the balance. Now many more firms favor entry through exporting, which permits broad and rapid coverage of world markets, reduces dependence on highly visible physical facilities, and offers much flexibility for making rapid adjustments. In terms of economies of scale and transaction costs, FDI is generally superior, but the risks of exporting are judged to be lower. Markets tend to punish failure more harshly than they reward success, which makes risk-minimizing strategies more effective.

Skillful management of global logistics and supply chains cuts the risk and cost of downtime. Firms seek closer relations with suppliers and clients to develop more trust and commitment. Some have increased "on-shoring" by bringing suppliers back into the country when their remoteness constitutes risk. Terrorism causes an organizational crisis whose ultimate effects may be unknown, and poses a significant threat to the performance of the firm. Corporate preparedness for the unexpected is a vital task. Innovative managers develop backup resources, and plan for dislocations and sudden shocks with a flexible corporate response.

Terrorism is a public threat, and some managers believe government should bear the cost of protecting against it. Others argue that a public–private partnership is the most effective approach, with firms taking the lead. There is also the issue whether corporate headquarters or the locally exposed subsidiary should fund prevention and preparation expenditures. Regardless of who pays, everyone can agree on the need to guard against terrorism.

Every world region is vulnerable, and most attacks are directed at businesses and business-related infrastructure. Terrorism requires decision making and behaviors that support vigilance and development of appropriate strategies. Managers who fail to prepare run the risk of weaker performance or even loss of the firm. While we can no longer choose the lowest cost option, 10 years after 9/11 companies are more aware, less exposed, and less vulnerable to the risk of terrorism. But in the next 10 years comes the really big task: What can and should we do collectively and individually to reduce the causes of terrorism.

CHAPTER 8

Hungary's Unacknowledged Leadership

OVI Magazine, May 2, 2016

Relative to population, Hungary has the
most Nobel Prize winners, but also the
most suicides. Linkage of coincidence?

Returning from Hungary, I was impressed by the breadth and depth of the courses offered by the Corvinus Hungarian Business School, which does not play second chair to U.S. universities. The admissions process, the scoring of applications, the transparency of decisions, and the competition for seats, were heartening indications of a market economy.

The country's strategic position in the heart of Europe, a highly developed logistics system, and traditional role as a trading post make it important as a regional production and distribution center. Porsche, General Motors, and Audi are now producing many of their cars in

Hungary—with other suppliers working for and around these popular firms. A recent investment by Mercedes Benz reaffirms the auto cluster formation in Hungary. The significant development of industries such as information technology, electronics, and automotive has attracted Foreign Direct Investment (FDI) at an ever-increasing rate. Hungary's acceptance as a member of the European Union as well as Schengen Zone further boosted its economic, social, and political development and stimulated more R&D activities.

All this is now jeopardized because of major EU internal strife over immigration policies. I observed the early stage of human flow between Serbia and Hungary, which was a 200-km-long green zone. Groups of 30 to 50 women, children, and men slowly walked across the border. The local chief of police shrugged, since he neither had the manpower nor the physical resources to round up or process the waves of humanity. In 2015, more than 400,000 people entered Hungary from Serbia. They aimed to settle in Germany, France, or Britain. The march through Hungary used to encounter an ostrich policy of "carry on and ignore." But the people who immigrate were worn out and not any less hungry because they were in Hungary. To rest, or feed themselves, they trespassed on property and took fruits and food. Locals were weary and talked about organized protection for their harvest. Growing pressures and complaints risk sparks in a tinder box.

The government of less than 10 million Hungarians has only limited resources to respond the clashes. A wall has been built to stop the immigration flow across the most accessible border areas. The public response in Europe to Hungary's defensive measures have been complaints, accusations of government over its reaction, and lack of sympathy toward the conflict. Proactive steps need to be accompanied by targeted help from abroad. Prime Minister Orban, a democratically elected head of government, was accused of a lack of sentimentality and guilty of behavior like a political winner (DUH)!

Hungary is again encountering its traditional environmental ambiguity. For centuries, the country has been too far east to be part of the West, and too far west to be integrated into the East. Throughout its history, there have been long-term occupations by the Tatars, Ottomans, and Austrians. The treaty of Trianon removed large portions of Hungary's population and resources. During the Cold War, Hungary kept conditions at least lukewarm with its Gulyas communism, and was often at the forefront of clamoring for change, for example, with its 1956 revolution against the Soviet Union, and the opening of its borders to escaping East Germans.

Again Hungary has been an early proponent of the need to monitor access to a country for purposes of justice, information planning, and control. Given its small size and population, repercussions of new factors are simply felt more quickly and demand more rapid actions, when compared to nations which have lots of reserve resources to deal with new conditions—although even those are eventually cognizant of the need for change.

Accusing the Hungarians of inhumanity for their regulation of migration is not very wise. To help or protect nations from the onslaught of humanity, walls have been built already 2000 years ago—just think of the Roman emperor Hadrian or the Chinese Qin Shi Huang. Walls are still being built today, just observe Austria, Serbia, and Turkey. Doing so is not a disregard for human lives, but rather an institutional requirement for control and the distribution of resources. Even Herculean efforts to provide food, shelter, and security for migrants can fail unless there is a timely count and assessment of human needs and the directionality of the massive flow of people.

It has not been sensible to overburden Hungary with expectations and demands for accommodative actions which, as we can see now, can even shake up major players. In today's times, leaders are all-too-often confronted with asymptotic conditions, where they encounter demands for actions by outsiders who are neither shouldering the political burden nor are paying for all their wonderful suggestions. Later on, those who earlier decried and dismissed responsible government, turned out to even imitate. Particularly in groups of nations which are often shaken by disagreement to demanding policies, one winds up with the unfortunate constant of politics: no gratitude, no memory, no long term, no acknowledgement of leadership: just like an unhappy couple.

SECTION II
International Innovations

CHAPTER 9

International Marketing After Macro Disruption (with Margit Enke)

Marketing Management, January 2016

**In Schumpeter's creative destructionism –
who bears the greatest burden?**

On rare occasions, we are given the opportunity to observe how macro changes in the international marketing environment result in adjustments in marketing content, application, context, and acceptance. One can begin to understand the marketing and societal implications by tracing major geopolitical shifts in history, such as the dissolution of the

Ottoman Empire and the Soviet Union, and the fusion of North and South Vietnam. In terms of forecast, one can track the present as well as the medium- and long-term futures of countries like the two Chinas, North and South Korea, Cuba, and Iran, to plan for substantial market and marketing-oriented changes that they may well undergo.

The reunification of West and East Germany provides a particularly prominent example of such a disturbance in the geopolitical equilibrium of the world. West Germany's willingness to invest grand sums in the market-based approach resulted in a reduction in the resource constraints faced by East Germany. Many of the economic differences in the two "zones" of Germany were the result of sharp divides in market perspectives. A review of the changes that took place is particularly timely now, in the 25th year of German reunification, where an entire new generation exposed to market interactions, orientations, and rules has arisen. One can now also witness the effect of these changes on population groups—effects that appear to differ systematically based upon the earlier political orientation of the German state in key areas such as migration policy, employment programming, education planning, and their repercussions on marketing.

The responses to changes also allow us to learn about marketing's role in the cohesion of society. Highlighting contrasts let marketing and its implications pop out in their perspective, and provide us with lessons for future plans. They also let us consider how to achieve further improvements in international marketing, linking the field with the newly emergent "curative marketing" approach. This approach advocates the fulfillment of the field's mission as a social science: to improve life and society, and restore and develop economic and spiritual health for all. We shall offer thoughts on the marketing environment, both as an influence on consumer behavior as well as a condition influenced by consumers, advertising, and purchasing decisions.

Environment and Consumer Behavior

Local East German marketers were thinly sewn, and their products faced a Herculean task after the Berlin Wall suddenly collapsed in 1989. Companies and products that had been protected by 60 years of state planning now had to face global, particularly West German, competition within 12 months. Those companies that did not go bankrupt immediately were often taken over by Western companies. However, these new owners sometimes feared intracompany competition, and terminated their East German products, even if they were better than their Western competition. The decomposition of the ecologically friendly Foron refrigerator from East Germany provides only one example.

Often, East German products failed to be introduced in the purchasing plans of most Western supermarkets and retailers. Then there was the carving of tight budgets. Market shares of all East German products dropped after reunification, since people switched to West German products for their novelty and better quality. "Western" products also seemed to have a certain aura that was traditional of the Eastern provinces but carried the whiff of East Germany's ancient socialist regime. It is interesting that now the East German identity is again tied much more to products, and again provides a strong emotional connection that encourages descendants of erstwhile East Germans to consume products from their home region. In the last two decades, some East German products experienced an unexpected revival. The "good old things" from a not-too-distant past are now considered fashionable or hip, and many producers are using this wave of Eastern reminiscences to relaunch and expand their brands.

Typical Macroeconomic Consumer Behavior Influences

German population statistics tell us that within 25 years, the five former East German states (excluding Berlin as a city-state) experienced a population decline of four million, with most of the young, female and educated population heading west. In 1991, every tenth citizen in the region was over 65 years old; it is now every fourth. Eastern unemployment figures improved from 18 to 12 percent, but are still considerably higher than the 6 percent of the Western provinces.

When marketing entered and penetrated the Eastern German economy, many East German companies went bankrupt. Some regions never recovered from the breakdown of the socialist system. With the exception of a few municipalities in Dresden, Leipzig, and Berlin, most consumers in Eastern Germany still have to budget with an average available income below 18,000 Euros, which reflects only 80 percent of the Western German average of 23,000 Euros. This comprises the conditions of the treaty agreed upon with Chancellor Kohl in 1990. The gap is also visible in terms of the monthly income for employed citizens. German citizens living in the Eastern provinces, regardless of their origin in the East or West, earn 25 percent less per month than their Western counterparts.

The relatively high unemployment rate and an aging population influence the consumption patterns in former East Germany by, for example, leading to a popularity of discounts. East Germans are also using a more differentiated pool of criteria when making purchasing decisions. In spite of the gap in consumption expenditure per capita, overall consumption patterns in the East and West are becoming increasingly similar. Private households in both parts of Germany spend the biggest proportion of their income on housing (East: 34.2 percent; West: 34.5 percent). The next largest expenditure is on transportation (East: 13.9 percent; West: 14.3 percent). Only the category, "food, beverages, and tobacco," presents a slight difference, of only 1.1 percent (West: 13.6 percent; East: 14.7 percent).

There are almost no differences in the frequency with which people go shopping for consumer goods. East- and West-Germany are similar in terms of shopping day and time preferences. Differences exist in how often consumers go to supermarkets—Eastern Germans usually prefer only one big purchase a week, whereas Western Germans prefer two, in order to take advantage of the biweekly advertising cycle.

Consumption Behavior and Attitude

Advertisement and Purchasing Decision

Germans living in the former German Democratic Republic (GDR) have a different attitude toward marketing in general and advertising in particular. While most West Germans are used to the ubiquitous noise of sensational promises by product advertisement—beer makes you more attractive and smoking a cigarette turns you into a free and manly cowboy—East Germans were raised in a less glitzy environment.

For them, advertisement had and still has an informative component. East Germans use it to compare and explore options before going to the supermarket and making the purchase. They were disillusioned and felt slightly betrayed when the promises of a product, for example, looking like a model after eating chocolate bars, did not materialize (Springer and Czinkota, 1999). This revelation came as a shock especially immediately after the reunification, when Western products and their advertisement flooded the former socialist state.

Promotion and Products

Household Appliances

On the product level there are still visible differences, especially in large white and brown goods. For example, only every fifth household in the Eastern provinces has a dryer (22.2 percent), while 43.8 percent have one in the West. Less dramatic but still major is the difference in terms of refrigerators. 40.9 percent have them in the East, and 53.1 percent have them in the West, the newspaper "Die Zeit" reports. For dishwashers, the numbers are 59.4 percent in the East and 69.5 percent in the West). Eastern German households have as many microwaves (71.8 percent) as their Western counterparts (72.7 percent). Eastern German households have caught up with their Western counterpart in terms of telephones (West: 99.8 percent; East: 99.8 percent), which is impressive when one takes into consideration that 20 years ago only every second household in the GDR had a phone. Today it is hard to imagine living without a telephone even in your house. At the same time, four out of five East German provinces are under the national average in terms of household Internet access. There is also a significant difference in Internet usage, where all five Eastern provinces are far below the German average.

Buyers and Brands

Today, the overall popularity of brands from Eastern Germany is increasing. However, there is only one product from the territory of the former GDR—a fine sparkling wine named "Rotkäppchen"—which made it to the Top Ten of most popular German brands in Western and Eastern Germany. Especially in the field of alcoholic beverages, Eastern products are getting stronger and more recognizable (e.g., Radeberger, Hasseröder, Köstrizer). More important, Eastern products are overcoming the old stereotypes of being of low quality and cheap. Nowadays, both Eastern and Western German consumers describe their local brands as being "trustworthy," "iconic/hip" (Ostalgie), and "likable."

At the same time, producers of Eastern German products can count less and less on Eastern German patriotism as a defining characteristic of customer behavior. Studies show that local patriotism is a much stronger factor for consumers older than 40 years of age than for those who are younger. Half of the over 40-year-old East German consumers would prefer Eastern German products, while this is only the case in a quarter of the 18- to 29-year age group. The producers need better marketing strategies to keep this younger generation of consumer close to their products.

Conclusion

The reunification of East and West Germany serves as an example of macro disruption. It shows how marketing environment has changed in terms of marketing content, application, context, and acceptance.

- With the dissolution of the socialistic regime, marketing contents changed. Western products and advertisements flooded the Eastern market and confused East German consumers. While advertisement in East Germany was rather informative, West German advertisement was rather glitzy and had the function of a sales strategy.
- Also adjustments in marketing application had to be made. East and West German consumers differ in their consumption patterns, which has to be considered by marketing strategies. These strategies should further aim at a better distribution of Eastern products in Western provinces.
- Since the fall of the Berlin Wall, marketing has taken place in a new context. East German products had to compete not only with West German products but also in a global context.

- Although people in Eastern Germany switched to the newer and higher quality products of West Germany, marketing acceptance was lacking because of sensational promises that were made but often did not come true.

Differences in unemployment rates, average available income, or the frequency of purchase are just a few topics international marketing has to address after a major market disruption. But there is one further topic that is of central importance—the shift in values. The reunification of East and West Germany as well as other conflicts, like the rapprochement of China and Taiwan or the Shiites and Sunnites, are examples of the slow process of value adaption. The parties concerned will be split for long time regarding social values. In this context, it is the objective of international marketing not to work on a global adaption of cultures, but to work on the acceptance or at least tolerance of foreign value systems.

Not solely the conflicts between countries or cultures have an impact on international marketing, but also the actions that occur out of them. The latest attacks in Paris are just one example of regularly terrorism that shocks the world and leads to a change of people´s views about international relations. The political instability influences not only international trade relations, but also the cohesion of society. One can speak of a general state of panic, and in this context of a global crisis of trust. Associations toward the responsible countries are transferred to the brands and products that originate from these countries. In the sense of making amends for past mistakes, the challenge of international marketing can be seen in "curative marketing." Creating international health as well as improving overall wellbeing may be the next marketing direction. It is the objective of international marketing to eliminate political prejudices and to give back safety. International marketing serves as a chance to build economic relationships that, in the end, restore political as well as social trust.

Due to these ongoing shifts in society and the general environment caused by macro disruptions, international marketing has changed and will be changing. In this context, we can observe some principal findings of international marketing after major market disruptions:

First, there is no shortcut for change and its acceptance. Eastern and Western Germany essentially presented optimal conditions in terms of available funding, ability to transfer funds, and willingness of the population to adapt. Nonetheless, one generation later we can still observe key differences from both a geographic perspective, where the East has remained more socialist in its orientation than the West, and also from an age perspective, where different age groups vary in their desire and success of leaving politics and socialism behind.

Second, there seems to be less willingness to accept differences across former boundaries, which can lead to disagreements of a substantial nature. The current debate about migration policies may serve as an example.

Observing the often hesitating processes of realignment, we should prepare for delays and disagreements with nations such as Cuba or Persia. Even with significant good will on all sides, the adjustments are slow and tedious. If enthusiasm is somewhat less exuberant, more delays and conflicts can be expected.

It is also noteworthy, however, that the success of a market orientation and of marketing thinking does, over time, typically improves lives and society. All this is likely to occur not by government fiat but by the choices devised and implemented by the private sector. The orientation for competition, risk taking, private property, and profit has enhanced life experience and life style—supporting the belief that self-actualization by taking one's own economic and marketing decisions can be the great reward for all.

CHAPTER 10

In Need of Honorable Merchants (with Kimberly Boeckmann)

Thunderbird International Business Review, August 2014

A powerful concept in today's international marketing field focuses on reestablishing honorable practices in the workplace and, more importantly, across borders.

The emphasis on the Honorable Merchant is a renewed issue in Europe, bringing fresh life to old thoughts. What exactly is an Honorable Merchant? It dates back at least to medieval history and ancient mercantile practices, where trust was paramount for achieving success. "Honorable practices" are rules established to guide merchants in conducting international business. For example, Berhold v. Regensburg admonished in 1210 that merchants should always use accurate measures and weights, highlighting honorable practices as a priority in society. These rules go all the way back to Proverbs (11:1), which specifically address merchants: "A false balance is an abomination to the Lord, but a just weight is his delight." The New Testament, Matthew 19:23–24, cites Jesus as saying "it is easier for a camel to go through the eye of a needle than for someone who is rich to enter the kingdom of God." Later on, the Quran resolves that charging interest is inappropriate and even sinful (Quran 3:130–131). In Chinese society, the role of a merchant was seen as a necessary evil, far below more exalted societal roles, such as imperial officials.

Honor also implied accountability beyond the merchants themselves, extending to their leaders. In the early 15th century, creditors from abroad requested that citizens convince their nobility to pay their trade debts. If not, they threatened attack not only on the noblemen and cities themselves, but also every merchant from those cities.

A summary then indicates:

a) The profession of merchants often has a dubious reputation, even more so internationally.

b) Mixed emotions are prevalent, since merchants can either help or hinder through their work.

c) Internationally, merchants may be at a disadvantage due to their foreignness. Their background and differences could detract from success in business.

d) International merchants are attractive as they bring choice to market; however, they still may displace domestic relationships.

e) To overcome this psychic distance, merchants must compensate for their shortcomings.

Merchants have long faced a variety of objections, making it difficult to climb the path to trust. Trust can facilitate investments in relationship assets, encourage information sharing, and lower transaction costs. However, honorable practices have developed over time, by building long-term customer relationships. We believe that the outcome of honorable behavior will be the construction of Trust Bridges.

An Honorable Merchant's reputation can be developed by highlighting commonalities and shared experiences, which establish a set of standards for international business. Exposing two parties to common conditions and values helps establish connectivity, warmth, and trust more rapidly than if they had no similar experiences. Through a combination of collaboration, symposia, conferences, and courses, partners can accredit and certify people or companies through a database of Trust Bridges.

In its annual Global Marketing conference, held recently in Cancun, the American Marketing Association sought to help in developing the Honorable Merchant concept. Today's critical characteristics of an Honorable Merchant must be to (1) build trust, (2) demonstrate corporate social responsibility (CSR), and (3) offer integrity and reliability, that is just because something can be done, the Honorable Merchant will not necessarily do it. All this needs to occur simultaneously in the realms of academia, business, and policy.

An essential application of a Trust Bridge exists for alumni of a university. A university's ability to establish an extraordinary environment enables the building of common bridges, anchored in similar life experiences. The most effective way to develop strong relationships is to highlight what each party brings to the table. Team work, networking, and reputation will increasingly become the main factor in choosing to attend a brick and mortar university, even after the Web and Internet provide alternatives to traditional education. However, for such efforts to be victorious, they must go beyond the mere transfer of information and help interested parties collaborate and connect.

Familiarity brings a fast track to relationships. A database of shared experiences can be instrumental in fostering such familiarity. A greater capacity for trust is developed through understanding, which shapes honorable relationships. Honorable practices should again become the expectation and norm.

CHAPTER 11

Shame Factor Can Curb Bad Behavior in Firms and Individuals (*with Shou Zhang*)

South China Morning Post, August 2015

Let us always remember our friends in prison.

As a researcher in international marketing issues at Georgetown University in Washington, DC, I am interested in the crackdown on indoor smoking implemented by the Beijing authorities.

Beijing has, for decades, been infamous for its heavy smog. Yet, outdoor air quality is not the only worry. Also of concern, but relatively more difficult for the government to monitor and control, is indoor air pollution, which is mainly caused by smoking.

To reduce the secondhand smoking risk, a new law came into effect on June 1. Anyone breaking these new regulations and policies will now face fines ranging from 200 Yuan (HK$250) for individuals to 10,000 Yuan for restaurants. Not only hitting with fines, repeat offenders will see their names posted on a government website for one month, alongside a list of their offences. A core dimension of the new law is public shaming. Witnesses to infractions are urged to notify the government. Social pressure can be exercised through shaming and is expected to make the new law more effective.

Shame could be used to get the attention of some "bad apples" causing headaches for the rest of us—especially when it comes to major collective action problems like climate change. It is just a matter of being creative and focused about choosing our targets.

Companies, such as British Petroleum or SeaWorld, do not experience guilt. However, the people working in these corporations do. Their thoughts and behavior can be influenced by public disapproval. Public opinion can be most essential for companies, especially if they are producing certain "brands," such as Apple with its iPhone. Reputational risks are a primary concern and public shaming is most effective if targeted at those corporations.

One must ponder the question: can "shame" really work in implementing government policy? Jennifer Jacquet, author of "Is Shame Necessary?", claims success for a website run by the state of California that lists the names of people who have not paid their taxes. The site targets only the top 500 delinquents, and the state has retrieved more than US$395 million in back taxes since it was launched in 2007.

Republican presidential candidate Jeb Bush advocates the use of shame as a tool, and says it should be used to reduce out-of-wedlock pregnancies. He believes that since people do not feel ashamed of single parenting, it has become OK for young women to give birth out of wedlock and young fathers to walk away from their paternal obligations.

Another possible and very helpful area for "shame policy" is immunization of a country's population. A society needs something like 90 percent of people getting vaccines for there to be true immunity. This obviously makes it easy for people to "free-ride" and opt out, since all the people around them are taking the needle for them. However, as soon as the state makes it easy for people to opt out, society gets down to 86 percent compliance and an immunization does not work anymore. That is why society needs regulation or some sort of shaming to reach that threshold, in order to make sure everyone safe.

Another example is the Rainforest Action Network and its shaming campaign against banks which were financially supporting coal companies doing mountain-top removal in the Appalachia region. After a five-year campaign, two of the nine banks have changed their policy to prevent the funding of coal companies. I'm not saying that this two out of nine is a major success, or even sufficient—hopefully someday this will be illegal. But it shows that shaming can act as a stop-gap for the period between when people are outraged about something and when there is actual legislation passed to stop it. These examples show how shame can be used to prevent certain behaviors in business and society.

Working to avoid shame can lead to better weights and measurements, a concern to avoid being ridiculed by competitors and losing one's long-developed reputation. Avoiding shame by reducing, eliminating, and making up for past mistakes can strengthen a company's unique selling proposition and let it emerge as a seasoned competitor.

Particularly in fields such as marketing, where the brand and personal perceptions are paramount, shaming can become a major influence if not the rationale for the curative approach leading to a healing of relationships between business, government, and consumers.

CHAPTER 12

Thoughts on the World Economic Forum

Sri Lanka Guardian, January 2015

Trade data are useful for general trends and
directions, not for their specific value.

The World Economic Forum (WEF) convened in Davos, Switzerland for a 4-day conference with more than 2,500 attendees, including government officials, politicians, and even some celebrities. With big names such as Angela Merkel, David Cameron, Jack Ma, and Bill Gates presenting their thoughts, the meeting is significant.

The WEF serves to expose new ideas and innovations and show "this is who we are, and that is what we need." It highlights the current and future issues and puts momentum behind sensitive international negotiations such as the Transatlantic Trade and Investment Partnership (TTIP) and the Trans-Pacific Partnership (TPP).

This year, the theme of the "new global context" focused on the conflicts instability, in addition to political, economic, and technological changes that make the world a fragmented place. The conference lived up to its reputation for insights and surprises such as the announcement that European Central Bank would purchase €60 billion a month to ward off deflation, encourage inflation and jumpstart growth across the 19 nations that are based off the Euro. Although many had expected smaller quantitative easing efforts, the annualized €720 billion was a reasonable comparison to the U.S. pumping in dollars in 2008 and 2009.

Canada's Prime Minister Justin Trudeau explained the work that went into unveiling the world's first 50/50 gender-balanced cabinet when he took power last year. It is a measure to encourage women to apply for public positions (since they represent 50 percent of the population). Meanwhile women still get paid less than men for the same work.

After years of tying the Swiss Franc to the Euro, the currency appreciated rapidly to its highest valuation in 30 years following the Swiss National Bank decision to allow an unrestricted rally of its currency.

A study released by international group Oxfam projects that the world's richest 1 percent, mostly from the United States and Europe, will soon own more than the rest of the world's population put together. Li Keqiang, Premier of the People's Republic of China, stated "we need to ensure a relatively high employment rate, especially sufficient employment for young people. And we need to optimize income distribution and raise people's welfare."

The number of people forcibly displaced in 2014 stood at 59.5 million according to the United Nations High Commissioner for Refugees (UNHCR), almost 50 percent more than in 1940.

Terrorism and its effect on the global economy were brought up by French president Francois Hollande. He mentioned, "there cannot be prosperity without security." Others called on the private sector to play a greater role in developing a global international response and addressing the root causes of terrorism.

Climate change, water crises, and social instability are seen as the greatest global risks for the next 10 years.

Personally, these three items surprised me:

- The lack of prepared plans and budgets for zero-cost money. Having free money not only expands the tools, but also changes the toolbox. This began in an era of mega trans-border problems, such as Ebola and climate issues, untold opportunities in space, and burdensome infrastructure reforms. All of these problems persist while the guests arrived in 1,700 private jets.
- Former Mexican President Calderon's claims that Mexicans in the United States do not want a new country, just more money. What an opening for public discourse and dissent!
- A lack of public pronouncements on the changing relationship with Cuba and its effect on all Caribbean competitors and their service industries. Just like Sherlock Holmes' non-barking dog, the attention given to the problems in Nigeria was insufficient.

As the meeting drew to a close, some big questions remain:

- With global problems in finance, growth, and health—who will run the show and who will give up sovereignty?
- What are the key tradeoffs, and who will supply the money?
- Are the key choices only between "feed, fund, or fight"? Is there a new role for humility and humanity?
- To what length should the daily "long-term" planning horizon of firms and government be recalibrated?
- Since trust is crucial, how can we encourage its growth and intensity, and which fields and endeavors should prioritize trust?
- Are there really long-term links between business and freedom?
- Is it time to slow down systematically, perhaps starting with "slow food"?

CHAPTER 13

Achieving "Glocal" Success (with Ilkka A. Ronkainen)

American Marketing Association, April 2014

Culture is inherently conservative. It resists change and fosters continuity.

Companies that have adopted this approach have incorporated the following four dimensions into their organizations.

Building a Shared Vision

The first dimension relates to a clear and consistent long-term corporate mission that guides individuals wherever they work in the organization.

Examples of this are Johnson & Johnson's corporate credo of customer focus; Coca-Cola's mission of leveraging global beverage brand leadership "to refresh the world, inspire moments of optimism and happiness, create value and make a difference"; Nestlé's vision to make the company the "reference for nutrition, health and wellness"; and Samsung's mission to "create superior products and services, thereby contributing to a better global society." But formulating and communicating a vision or mission cannot succeed unless individual employees understand and accept the company's stated goals and objectives.

Broadening Perspectives

This relates to the development of a cooperative mindset among region or country organizations to ensure the effective implementation of global strategies. Managers may believe that global strategies are intrusions on their operations if they do not have an understanding of the corporate vision, if they have not contributed to the global corporate agenda, if they are not given direct responsibility for its implementation, or if there is no reward for their cooperation.

Capable Managers

The third component in the "glocal" approach is making use of representatives from different countries, regions, and cultures. Organizationally, the forces of globalization are changing the country manager's role significantly. With profit-and-loss responsibility, oversight of multiple functions, and the benefits (and drawbacks) of distance from headquarters, country managers enjoyed considerable decision making autonomy, as well as entrepreneurial initiative. Today, however, many companies have to emphasize the product dimension of the product-geography matrix, which means that power has to shift at least to some extent from country managers to worldwide strategic business unit and product-line managers. Many of the previously local decisions are now subordinated to global strategic moves.

Internal Cooperation

In today's environment, the global business entity can be successful only if it is able to move intellectual capital within the organization—that is, to transmit ideas and information in real time. If there are impediments to the free flow of information across organizational boundaries, important updates about changes in the competitive environment might not be communicated in a timely fashion to those tasked with incorporating them into the strategy.

CHAPTER 14

Innovation in Developing Economies (with Ilkka A. Ronkainen)

Daily Egypt News, November 2014

Innovation in developing economies is evolving rapidly, but still can improve in terms of marketing. Businesses in emerging economies can make profits and can positively affect the livelihoods of people. In the next generation, multinational corporations can expand to vast unserved and underserved consumer groups in developing countries. Executives need to redefine their roles and relationships across companies and radically depart from traditional business models through new partnerships and structures.

Research

Businesses need to understand the aspirations and habits of target populations. For most emerging-market consumers, price is not the only determining factor, but rather the total purchase cost (including transportation cost, time, the burden of carrying purchases, and storage availability). Large U.S. chocolate companies established only a marginal presence in Latin America with their standard American large chocolate bars. In contrast, Arcor and Nacional de Chocolates have grown their businesses by selling more affordable bite-sized chocolates that are available in remote rural stores.

Digital Technology

Due to the economic and physical isolation of poor communities, businesses that provide access to digital technology have the potential to thrive. Cisco partners with a range of global and local partners to sell, lease, or donate $300 million worth of computer products and services to markets worldwide. In Bangladesh, where the average annual income is $200, GrameenPhone Ltd. leases access to wireless phones to villagers. Every phone is used by an average of 100 people and generates $90 in revenue per month—two or three times the revenue generated by wealthier users who own a phone in urban areas. This program has been replicated in other countries, including Uganda and Rwanda.

Financial Services

Microfinance programs have allowed consumers to borrow sums averaging $100 to make purchases without using collateral. The mission of microfinance is to let the poor access financial services and improve their living standards. For example, Te Creemos developed a complete electronic payment solution in Mexico by partnering with MasterCard, which affords small- and medium-sized enterprises a micro-business card and a low-cost payment method.

Local Solutions

Many emerging consumers do not shop at supermarkets. Nestlé employs local residents with pushcarts who take small quantities of merchandise to kiosks. Unilever is rolling out similar strategies in Kenya, Indonesia, Vietnam, and other countries offering five-peso "starter packs" in the Philippines. Others reach out to beachcombers via bicycles. Innovations can start in developing countries first, and disseminate via a trickle-up approach. Pepsi snacks like Kurkure and Aliva from India have attracted attention from the United Kingdom and the United States.

Distribution

In the past, underdeveloped and monopolistic distributing networks of developing countries saw their primary jobs as distributing sales literature, cutting through red tape, and charging invariably high fees. Today, outside competition has forced distributors to add value to what they do. If local conditions do not measure up, companies are willing to use outside captive distribution systems or to appoint their own people in place. Eveready has an extensive network of associates and 15 distributors who support its business in East.

Multinational Commitments

Businesses, governments, and civil societies can join together in a common cause to help the aspiring poor to join the world economy. Lifting billions of people from poverty may help avert social decay, political chaos, terrorism, and environmental deterioration. For example, Procter & Gamble has a Safe Drinking Water program in Kenya through their water-purifying brand PUR that improves access to safe drinking water. Coca-Cola funds "Slingshot," a water purification system for communities in need. Multinational companies can envision a world empowered by equal access to life's basic needs.

Challenge to Existing Business

Marketers need to convert innovation opportunities in developing countries. Historically, what worked for a peasant in rural Kenya or Colombia had little interest for a sophisticated urban consumer in the West. Now, these opportunities may provide new platforms for growth even in post-industrialized markets. Africa's prospects have proved alluring to Wal-Mart, which has agreed to pay roughly $2.4 billion to buy 51 percent of South Africa's Massmart Holdings, with plans to use the discount retailer for continental expansion. Yum Brands recently said it wants to double its KFC outlets in emerging countries over the next few years to 1,200. Rising consumption will increase the demand for local products, and, given proper support, will trigger domestic growth and lift developing countries and their consumers up to greater economic opportunity and a better life.

CHAPTER 15

How Companies Can Befriend a Trend (with M. Schrader)

American Marketing Association, February 2015

A rising tide may lift boats, but only if they are prepared and capably managed.

. . .Only if companies identify trends early on and draw the right conclusions. But what is a trend, and what are its consequences for multinational corporations?

Trend research is a booming business. Many agencies and self-appointed gurus announce their latest trends to generate publicity and awareness. This can be particularly confusing for MNCs: apart from local and regional trends they have to identify international and cross-regional trends and incorporate them into their strategic planning and decisions.

Companies must deal with trends and trend research. If they miss out on market developments which fundamentally change customer interactions, they are doomed to fail. Just think of Kodak's neglect of tectonic shifts in the photography market to its major detriment. Yet, misjudging a blip for a trend may cost a firm critical amounts of money and reputation. Even today people still cite the warning 1958 example of the Ford Edsel which, though leading edge in technology, did not appeal to buyers. On the other hand, a trend identification at an early stage can significantly help a firm to distinguish itself from competitors and to lastingly strengthen its brand. Toyota demonstrated this with the Prius. The Japanese carmaker realized early on that fuel efficiency and "green driving" is not only an ecologic necessity, but also a customer preference. That is why Toyota's decision to be the first to launch a hybrid car in mass production had such a positive impact on its brand image.

What Exactly Is a Trend?

Merriam-Webster defines it as "a line of movement and development or a prevailing tendency." This makes a trend not a future occurrence, but rather an event line which becomes apparent through current incidents which point into the same direction. The challenge is to filter out of a multitude of ambivalent incidents those who eventually will become a straight line of change. Single events do not make a trend, but may well mark the beginning of it and therefore need to be tracked.

Trends impact marketing actions in various ways: Product technology can be influenced and changed by a trend. Take electric mobility as a current example. The electric impulse in new automobiles differs fundamentally from the traditional fuel engine. Companies must acquire completely new technology competences in order to compete. In the electric car the energy storage in the battery is the decisive component. Those car companies which engaged full-fledged with this technology early on, acquired know-how and cooperated with partners, developed and maintained key competitive advantages.

Technology changes can also lead to different pricing models due to a change in cost structures. Particularly newly emerging competitors may develop entirely new pricing usance in an industry. A trend may influence the way MNCs interact with their clients, or lead to new customer needs and preferences. Trends can cause the development of new distribution or sales channels or lead to changes in the existing sales structure.

Technologic and Socio-cultural Trends Are Especially Relevant

Technological or socio-cultural changes in particular must be on the MNCs radar, since these shifts are most frequent and often most discontinuous in the international realm. Do new technologies emerge that entirely replace the existing product technology or functionality, such as, for example, driverless cars? Are there social changes, which point to new consumption needs or habits? Technology-driven companies and life-style firms, such as MNCs operating in the smart communication, automotive, or fashion business, are in special need of professionally organized trend research. This is especially true for firms in markets where consumer desires and preferences may change quickly. Pret A Manger, a global sandwich restaurant chain emanating from the UK, is constantly in search of new food trends by monitoring food blogs or visiting health shops. If a new ingredient becomes notably popular, it is rapidly considered in the firm's offering. Pret A Manger pays special attention to the timing of change introduction. "We have the most success at the middle of the curve," a company spokeswoman recently told the Wall Street Journal.

In our experience it is not a lack of trend information, which is problematic. To the contrary, many large MNCs have a significant amount of trend-relevant data. But there is a lack of a comprehensive and systematized data analysis, extraction, and condensation. Such steps, however, are crucial for identifying sustainable international marketing strategies.

MNCs need trend scouts or trend specialists who deal with trends in their respective domain. Specific employees will be responsible for trend research in Marketing, in R&D, in manufacturing, and so on. This allocation is necessary because business functions have become so special-ized that in order to furnish meaningful analyses, trend researchers need to be grounded in specific field. While outsourcing of trend research to third-parties, may make sense in widely diverse markets, the interpreta-tion of data and events needs to be done by the MNC itself, if it wants to identify a trend early, recognize the cross sections between trends, func-tions and corporate activities and use these insights to generate a competi-tive advantage.

If trend research is split between parts of the organization, it requires a mechanism that consolidates, compares, and jointly interprets the work and insights of the different trend specialists. A Head of Trend Research as coordinator should oversee the firm-wide activities in the single lines of business. That person should also ensure at the 'C' level within the firm that there is corporate follow-up, including investment decisions using the trend findings.

Standardization Versus Adaptation and Its Effect: A Trend Research

Trend research is no easy task. It is ambitious and requires considerable resources. The challenge is even bigger for MNCs because they need to recognize and distinguish between local, regional, and global trends. For example, how does one understand whether a particular phenomenon is a singular aberration or a "black swan" presaging an entirely new context, and how are insights communicated best within the firm? It becomes important to understand whether an MNC's marketing program is stan-dardized across regions or whether it is adapted to and from local pref-erences or requirements. If standardized, the MNC perceives customer preferences as identical across the world, thus pursuing a homogeneous marketing program and a global product. In this case, the MNC tends to turn its focus toward global trends, looking for application in a diversity of markets.

If the marketing program is adapted, the research scope requires to be differentiated, that is trends need to be researched on a region- and market-level. As MNCs are usually active in several foreign countries, firms following the "adaptation" approach typically develop trend research targets will be those markets of special importance, based on revenue, profit, or strategic considerations. For most European MNCs for example, China will be on top of the list.

Strengthening One's Trend Research Capability

One of the major decisions in international marketing concerns the entry mode used to conquer a new market. The options range from simply shipping to foreign customers (direct export) to licensing and, finally, the complex and resource-intensive establishment of own subsidiaries. The entry mode choice has implications on the trend research capability. If the MNC is not active in the foreign market (as in the case of direct exporting or licensing), reliable trend research for this market is quite difficult. Dependence on secondhand information makes for with a difficult interpretation due to a lack of local market knowledge. The more engaged the MNC is, the easier it is to interpret events early on and to identify a trend. Only presence in a foreign market enables to gain local (trend) know-how. That is why many Western MNCs should exploit their recently built-up Sales and Research & Development capacities in emerging markets for trend research purposes.

Much work done on trend identification suffers from key drawbacks. One is the limitation of the work to one country only, even though trends are often a global phenomenon. Often one can sense that the time is ripe for a change, but the actual shift may occur in a variety of countries. Unless there is good awareness of diverse markets, one risks losing out on the trend signals. A second shortcoming concerns the constituencies of the international marketing process. Even though trends in international marketing are driven by the interaction of the business, policy and scientific communities, firms typically query only one group of these players. In consequence, the insights obtained are limited to the views of the one group investigated, and do not reflect the important and possibly different perspectives of the two groups left out. It is important to have trend research reflect the interaction between the business, policy, and scientific communities to obtain reasonably accurate and calibrated insights into impending metamorphoses. Twenty years of research on trends conducted by us have shown that the use of such a differentiation into these three communities has generated an average trend forecasting accuracy of 76 percent.

It is now time to pay attention to the importance of trend research for competitive international business strategies. If MNCs start to systematize their trend research and align their trend research scope and capability with their product strategy and do so across different constituencies, then the trend may well become their very best friend.

CHAPTER 16

Eagles Fly But Don't Always Soar

Liechtensteiner Vaterland, Spring 2008

A sharp vision has varied effects.

The world's stock markets experience a decline. Sharp drops of shares occurred in Hong Kong, Istanbul, and Frankfurt, and many seem to blame the United States and the market approach as the causes for their predicament. Commentators now predict a serious global recession for all markets. The United States is singled out with additional forecasts promising a steep drop of the U.S. dollar, sharp reductions in U.S. military strength, and vanishing of U.S. political influence. Alas, these commentators are sadly mistaken.

All too often, forecasters are looking only at the short term. Their long term usually means next week. Yet, the world turns much slower than the typical media blurb makes us believe. Countries adjust their strategies only gradually, as do most customers, entrepreneurs, and corporations. Rather than being driven by momentary shifts, sensible thinkers search for a context, and look at the road rather than the turnoff. Take the current changes in share values. Financial markets have changed for many years—and typically, in the past few decades, it has been for the better. Families, towns, provinces, and nations have improved their lot. Health care has improved, both in terms of pharmaceuticals and in care delivery. Housing has become better, and education, a crucial ingredient of progress and growth, now reaches many more than ever before. Incomes are strong.

Today, there is much more ability to achieve, accomplish, and to accumulate. There is less famine, more opportunity, and more freedom. Life is best it's been in millennia. It is human nature to strive upward and therefore not be satisfied with the *status quo*. But such a drive should concentrate not just on a few select economic issues of the moment. We have even come to the point where mere stability and constancy are seen as wrong and as indicative of "falling behind." Imagine an executive who told his shareholders that he wants his company's sales to remain stable—most analysts would probably run him over on their way to other firms. But isn't stability in itself worthwhile and good? What ever happened to catching one's breadth! As children, many of us read stories and books about "getting ready for a rainy day." By doing so, there was no implication that temporary setbacks were a fatal disease. Rather, there was an acceptance, forged from experience with Mother Nature that there are seasons, and that life has its ups and downs. Even eagles occasionally descend to lower heights so that they can catch an updraft and soar again. There is nothing to be ashamed of if resources have to be rearranged and if one accepts that not everything is linear. Think of growth in the context of angles on a protractor: Growth does not always have to take place at all degrees, on all levels, and simultaneously.

For those who see the United States and the benefits of the market approach which it has propagated, in steep decline, let them look at history, as sensible people do. For example, in a recent discussion of global economics, a Chinese acquaintance readily agreed that his nation had perhaps had a bad run which lasted a century, but he assured me that China was now ready to again become the center of the world. Think of the long-term and ongoing contributions of the United States to world economic growth and welfare. In the 1940s, the country pioneered the three key international organizations which form the pillars of world trade and investment: The International Monetary Fund (IMF), the World Bank, and the World Trade Organization (WTO). Without them, the world economy could never have reached its current level of success. Through joint efforts on the exchange rate front and a willingness to rely on market-based exchange rates, the United States ensured growing money supply which has led to rising economic abundance. The country's willingness to be the largest marketplace to the world has provided opportunities for innovation, growth, profit, and enjoyment to many. And all this has been achieved within a system that provides for political adjustments and transitions without unchecked power, bloody battles, or economic destruction.

The United States remains the land of opportunity where one can realize dreams under open skies. It continues to be a key destination for immigrants, because they know that vision is admired, that effort is rewarded, and that achievement is supported. There is security and safety in the land, and there is flexibility to adjust to new conditions. Even in times of temporary setbacks, the outlook is bright. Trust, promise, and the future that a nation offers to those holding its investments, its currency, and its contracts are the long-term key dimensions which define global leadership. Those who believe that the United States is in terminal decline should remember that the Roman Empire lasted more than 700 years, the Ottoman Empire almost 600, Britain's for 350 years. They too had their ebb and flow, and they demonstrated that good expectations for the longer-term future together with internal cohesion provided sufficient impetus for continuing success. The best is yet to come.

SECTION III

International Marketing and Freedom

CHAPTER 17

Why International Marketing strengthens Freedom

Congressional Records US House Representatives, May 2005

Plaques, bonuses or medals. Which do you prefer and why?

You may ask what freedom has to do with international marketing. Freedom is about options. If there is no alternative, there is no freedom. A true alternative provides the opportunity to make a decision, to exercise virtue. In the blaze of the klieg lights, it is easy to make the "right" decision. That is not an exercise in virtue, because real alternatives are effectively removed. The true selection among alternatives takes place in the darkness of night when nobody is looking.

The focus and aim of international marketing is on crossing borders. The goal is to provide more than one choice for customers, letting them pick from a selection of options in order to maximize their satisfaction. International marketing does so in all corners of the globe, the glamorous ones as well as in the small and remote ones where the efforts are not seen by others. By operating both in the limelight and also well outside of it, international marketing offers the freedom to exercise virtue both to the seller and the buyer—be it in decisions of supplying or purchasing, pricing or selecting.

Another key dimension of freedom is not to confine, but allow people to go outside of the box. As a concept, freedom knows no international boundaries. But national borders usually are the boxes where business and government find their limits. Such borders are a mere point of transition for international marketing. The discipline thrives on understanding of how to successfully cross national borders, on coping with the differences once the crossing is done, and on profitably reconciling any conflicts. International marketing contains the freedom of almost unlimited growth potential. Activities confined to domestic borders may well run into limits of expansion.

International market opportunities relax these limits quickly. Instead of restrictions, the international marketing paradigm encourages the stripping away of restraints; instead of limitations, there is the encounter of wide opportunity. Hayek thought that freedom also means not being forced to do something one does not want to do. There are economic migration pressures that force people to move from their rural homes into urban areas, from their developing countries into industrialized ones or from wartime conditions to peaceful environment. Industrialized nations, in turn, speak about immigration pressure. For both sides, little if any freedom is involved here. Most individuals who do the moving would much rather stay home but cannot afford to do so due to major exigencies. The recipient countries might not want to welcome the migrants but do so in response to political and humanitarian pressures.

International marketing may have been part of what triggered some of these migrations, but it also can be instrumental in stemming the tide. It can provide the economic opportunity for individual at home so that they need not migrate. Thus, it lets individuals become productive contributors to the global economy free from pressures to shift locations. When the long-standing rivalry between socialism and market orientation was resolved, market forces and the recognition of demand and supply directly affected human rights and the extent of freedom. With all humility and gratefulness, we can conclude: Markets were right! In country after country, market forces have demonstrated typically greater efficiency and effectiveness in their ability to satisfy the needs of people. International marketing has been instrumental in stimulating these newly emerging market forces. In spite of complaints about the slowness of change, biases in wealth distribution, and the inequities inherent in societal upheavals, a large majority of participants in market-oriented conditions are now better off than they were before. Without the transition provided by international marketing, these changes would not have come about that swiftly and efficiently.

One keeps healing about the large segment of the world population that is poor and therefore supposedly excluded from any international marketing efforts; the World Bank calls them the 3 billion $3-a-day poor. By contrast, international marketers should see them as an attractive $9 billion-a-day opportunity for valuable transactions. What is more is that international marketing provides the opportunity to acquire resources without the deployment of force. Why fight if you can trade? Countries that have been historic enemies such as France, England, and Germany are now all united in collaboration through international marketing. The field is, therefore, at the very least contributing to freedom from war while providing additional choices and freedom for consumption.

CHAPTER 18

The Cost and Obstacles for Freedom

Congressional Record US House Representatives,
May 2005

The cost of freedom is rising. Terms like free trade or free choice are misleading since they all come with a price, which international marketers pay in terms of preparing their shipments, scrutinizing their customers, and conforming to government regulations. We all are paying a higher price due to global terrorism.

As freedom suffers, so does international marketing. In most instances, terrorism is not an outgrowth of choice but rather the lack of it. Terrorists may succeed in reducing the freedom of others but not in increasing their own. Who is typically most affected by terrorist acts? Attacks aimed at businesses, such as the infamous bombings of U.S. franchises abroad, do not bring big corporations to their knees. The local participants, the local employees, the local investors, and the local customers are affected most.

Who can protect themselves against such attacks and who can afford to protect targets? Only the wealthier countries and companies can. They have the choice of where to place their funds, with whom to trade, and whether to hold the enemy at bay through a security bubble created by changing business formats via exporting or franchising. The poor players do not have choices. The local firms, the nations with developing economies, and the poor customers continue to remain exposed to further acts of terrorism with very limited indigenous ability to influence events.

But international marketing can enable the disenfranchised to develop alternatives. Multinational firms can invest in the world's poorest markets and increase their own revenue while reducing poverty. With support from shareholders and the benefit of good governance, international marketers can, and should, continue in their role as social change agents. The discipline has value maximization at its heart. If it is worthwhile to fulfill the needs of large segments of people, even at low margins, then it will be done. International marketers after all have as their key desire the creation of new customers, suppliers, and markets. They are delighted when, in fulfillment of their aims, they can bring about freedom from extremes of hunger, sickness, and intolerance.

In a global setting, freedom can take on many dimensions. Privileges and obligations that are near and dear to some may well be cheap and easily disposed of by others. The views of one society may differ from views held in other regions of the world. Such differences can account for misunderstandings, surprises, and long-term conflicts. There are two value dimensions at work here, both of them highly relevant to international marketing. One may be circumscribed as the freedom and values of a market economy. To make them work, governmental, managerial, and corporate virtue, vision, and veracity are required. Until the world can believe in what institutions and their leaders say and do, it will be difficult to forge a global commitment between those doing the marketing and the ones being marketed to.

It is therefore of vital interest to the proponents of freedom and international marketing to ensure that corruption, bribery, lack of transparency, and poor governance are exposed for their negative effects in any setting or society. The main remedy will be the collaboration of the global policy community in agreeing on what constitutes transgressions and on swift punishment of the culprits involved, so that market forces can work free from distortion.

A second and even more crucial issue is the value system we use in making choices. Some years ago, the Mars Climate Orbiter mission failed spectacularly as a result of the use of different values by the mission navigation teams. One team was using metric units and the other used the English system of measurement. This mistake caused the orbiter to get too close to the atmosphere, where it was destroyed.

There are major differences among what people value around the world. Contrasts include togetherness next to individuality, cooperation next to competition, modesty next to assertiveness, and self-effacement next to self-actualization. Often, global differences in value systems keep us apart and result in spectacularly destructive differences. How we value a life, for example, can be crucial in terms of how we treat individuals. What value we place on family, work, leisure time, or progress has a substantial effect on how we see and measure each other.

Cultural studies tell us that there are major differences between and even within nations. International marketing, through its linkages via goods, services, ideas, and communications, can achieve important assimilations of value systems. On the consumer side, new products offer international appeal and encourage similar activities around the world: many of us wear denim, dance the same dances, and eat pizza and sushi. It has been claimed that local product offerings help define people and provide identity. Johansson states that is the local idiosyncrasies that make people beautiful. Some even offer the persistence of the specific breakfast habits of the English and the French as evidence of local immutability in the face of globalization. Yet, we should remember that values are learned, not genetically implanted. As life's experiences grow more international and more similar, so do values. Therefore, every time international marketing forges a new linkage in thinking, new progress is made in shaping a greater global commonality in values. International marketing's ability to align global values which makes it easier for countries, companies, and individuals to build bridges between them, may eventually become the field's greatest gift to the world.

How do freedom and international marketing match with today's discontent so forcefully expressed by the disgruntlement of the anti-globalists? Many claim that never before in history has there been so much evidence about such strong opposition to globalization and to Americans as harbingers of international marketing. Perhaps those making such claims are sadly mistaken. In looking at other "globalizers" in world history, such as the Vikings, the Mongols, the Tatars, and the Romans, there probably was both intellectual and physical opposition (or do we really believe that everybody enjoyed Genghis Khan?). But protest was never allowed to become very vocal, or to engage in repeated, large demonstrations or widespread pamphleteering. Due to rather harsh policies of dealing with the opposition, very few records of such resistance are available today. Consequently, comparisons with past events are difficult to make and are likely to be highly inaccurate.

Today's news is good. The nations, institutions, and individuals around the world are increasingly accepting freedom as the key foundation of the good life. We are discovering that international marketing, both as a discipline and as an activity, is very closely interwoven with freedom—some even call it essential. It is the freedom Thomas Aquinas saw as the means to human excellence and happiness, which international marketing helps us reach. In reciprocal causality, freedom causes and facilitates international marketing, while international marketing is a key support of the cause of freedom. A productive symbiosis at work!

CHAPTER 19

Parallel Parking and National Security

OVI Magazine, June 2015

When they are "generally speaking", better
report with: " yes sir".

The other day the local news reported that the state of Maryland has dropped parallel parking from its driver's test. A Maryland spokesperson explained that the requirement is "redundant" with other tests. However, parallel parking separates the wheat from the chaff. Most people who fail the test do so because of the parallel parking burden. From now on, without such requirement, more people will pass the test. A triumph of better driving? I don't think so!

More licenses do not mean that new drivers are more capable. The test is only an indicator for what is being tested. Dropping elements of a test may simplify a process but may not contribute to safer roads. If parallel parking is "redundant" and the skills are already included in other requirements, how come people fail the redundant part? If a student knows the answer to 1+2 but not to 3+5, can the math teacher pass that student? Imagine the consequence of allowing unqualified drivers on the road. This is much more serious than failed math students doing cashier work.

In other countries, such as Germany, the driver's license costs up to $ 1,800 Euro with mandatory evening (theory) lessons and 18 hours of mandatory driving practice. Parallel parking is seen as an integral part of the training, even or because it is the most feared part in the teenagers day-to-day driving. Other lectures include night driving, inner city driving, and driving at 100 to 125 mph at the federal highways (there is no speed limit at German highways) to prepare the students for their real experience as drivers without an instructor on their side.

Young drivers under 20 years have crash rates 3 times those of the average American driver per each mile. Immaturity leads to speeding and other risky habits, and inexperience means young drivers often do not know how to react in certain situations. From a purely rational risk averting standpoint we should give our teenagers the training they need to master the traffic and to be mindful citizens in the streets. Striking challenging requirements of the list does not change reality and will not make our streets safer or our teenagers' better drivers.

The debate of continuing the National Security Agency's telephone metadata collection program for terrorism surveillance is similar. It has been argued for years whether the program contributes to national security at a price of privacy concerns. Can the program's insights really prevent terrorist attacks when terrorists and their supporters use a medley of communication tools? For example, whatsApp, SnapChat, RedPhone are new communication methods which do not rely on phone lines but rather on Internet connections. Can government interception stay ahead of the game? Not to mention that terrorists may ride motorcycles to pass along information without using any hi-tech tools. Should we monitor every motorcycle for national security? It is comforting to see that the House has passed a bill to end NSA's collection of domestic phone metadata, while substituting case-by-case searches for national security concerns.

Back to driving: The new test makes unqualified drivers' lives easier, but it also takes away options from them as well. It is similar to the problem of drivers experienced only with automatic shifts rather than those experienced with a manual transmission. Drivers trained on automatic cars only may have great difficulty driving safely in Europe when they get a car with a manual transmission, which is typical for rentals. More skills can help us handle more kinds of situations, and therefore, make our life and that of others easier.

Technologies such as backup cameras may help drivers prevent careless accidents. But expected advanced technology that can make driving easier, such as self-driving vehicles is, far from maturity. Nowadays, we tend to rush into the result of innovations to the detriment of established technology. When I first moved into our newly built building about 5 years ago, the building was beautiful with thin TVs on the walls, automatic doors, and light control sensors. However, many electrical outlets did not work.

In summary, the comfortable and easy way may be paved with good intentions, be it for learning how to drive or learning how to listen. Of course we should support innovations with good intent, but future ease may not yet work well with current reality. During the gap from now to fully adequate automation, we still need to learn how to drive and park safely, and how to intercept accurately.

CHAPTER 20

Too Much Information for Germans and Americans

Sri Lanka Guardian, May 2015

The intelligence communities on both sides of the Atlantic (and probably the Pacific too) are reeling. Major accusations are levied about the inappropriateness and possibly even illegality of their data-collection efforts. Going far beyond the Edward Snowden revelations, the claim is about systematic industrial espionage, with data scooping far in excess needed for the battle against terrorism. German chancellor Merkel Germany is accused of either having approved industrial espionage assistance provided to the United States by the German Federal Information Service, or of not having kept up with such assistance practices by Germany's secret trolls.

The accusations do not differentiate between the collection of information and the subsequent usage of the information. Information gathering is akin to panning for gold. One does not know what is there until one has it. Here can be indications, impressions, rumors, suggestions—but what matters in the end is what one actually has in hand.

Once information is available, the question becomes what to do with it. Here it is important to remember the purpose and rationale for the collection process, which can cover issues ranging from nuclear non-proliferation to safeguarding against terrorism, or tracking of potential attacks. There is temptation to think of secondary uses for new knowledge, particularly when it could be worth hard percentage points on the competitiveness scale, such as new insights on hydraulics, or new genetic understandings of agricultural production.

Such possible collateral data benefits, which were not (or should not have been) part of the original collection plan, represent high temptation for abuse, and can lead to an abyss of distrust. Once discovered, there is psychic distancing between governments, and growing legal uncertainty for firms who have received and used information. What may appear like a good deal now, may, in future lay the foundation for massive punitive payments which could lead to ruin.

New heydays for attorneys and notaries follow as well, since all sides want to be protected. Transactions slow down and become more expensive because counsel needs to be consulted and more participants provide input, for a price. Clandestine information inflow makes collaboration more difficult and reduces the ability to develop far-reaching visions. One cannot always attribute new insights to late-night eureka moments.

Just because something can be done does not mean that it should be done. Particularly in the international realm it is important, just as it was centuries ago, to be known as an Honorable Merchant whom others can trust and join in collaboration. On the German–American information collection side there are few problems: Reinhard Gehlen, Germany's spy chief of last century's fame, writes in his memoirs in the late 1960s about the permanent U.S. right to collect data in Germany. Even without any agreement, such sharing of insights is still reasonable today.

An analysis of the use of collected data (or lack thereof) can benefit from German literature. Franz Kafka's "The Trial" shows how nontransparent information in the hands of public authority can diminish humanity. Max Frisch in his "Arsonists" explains the danger from evildoers who are not restrained in their actions. Unless society is sensitive to these issues, otherwise, Frisch concludes, the house will burn.

Using information obtained for sovereign protective purposes to enhance corporate competitive advantage, is wrong. Doing so, distorts market signals to investors, producers, and customers. These signals provide free nations with economic superiority, capabilities, and innovation. Those who manage information on terrorists have no advantage in providing information to businesses.

Government actions can push firms in directions which they would not have taken, to everybody's detriment. We have seen such distortions for computer chips in the past, and in solar technology at present.

We live in an era of transition. Entirely new ways for information collection and use are becoming possible. We all have to learn to understand new conditions and expectations. The economic dimension is important but not the only dimension leading to societal and individual content. Those that collect, use, and distribute data must clarify their purpose at least internally, already early on obtain insights from data use specialists, and attain agreement on collaboration and then stick to the plan. Otherwise the benefits which look good now will come back to haunt us all later. The German and American governments and firms deserve better.

CHAPTER 21

Trust: A Tool to Defeat Corruption (with Courtlyn Cook)

Japan Today, January 2015)

Trust bridges are increasingly emphasized in business relations and partnerships. They not only help to fight corruption, but also establish a sense of community that binds people together. Corruption continues to be a hot issue in business and is more prevalent than most people acknowledge. The baseline standard of corruption, defined by the nonprofit

Transparency International, is an "abuse of entrusted power for private gain." The group sees corruption as the pursuit of selfish, individual gains and the desire to get ahead. Of course, corruption is an individual, as well as a corporate choice. Transparency International's latest study reports that 25 percent of people used a bribe in the past year, which means that corruption infiltrates a significant portion of business transactions, which is crucial to take into consideration. Corruption interrupts corporate culture because it destroys previously established trust that has been earned on a long-term basis.

Trust is a valuable corporate asset since it typically translates into fulfilled expectations, which allow for better forecasts, less uncertainty in the future, and more realism. Trust bridges, developed by shared expectations and experiences, allow people to get to know each other quicker, and help establish fair business practices on global terms. Thus, trust is one of the best ways to combat corruption. Connections that bring people together and lead to greater trust can be built upon a shared alma mater, military service, same work experience, sports fans for the same team, and even practicing the same religion. People are more likely to bond over these personal preferences and organizations because they already share a similar interest. Therefore, they expect to share similar values. If two companies operate in similar environments and share values, they are more likely to connect and establish warm and trusting relationships. This ultimately establishes credibility and allows business to select patterns based on trust rather than strictly on proximity or financial measures.

Trust is developed through interaction, although there are other spillover effects that come into play. An example would be two organizations that are led by former sports champions might be more likely to trust each other, particularly when it comes to sports. This may also connote, but does not necessarily require trust in financial matters. It is important to note that trust is an extension of confidence, so high expectations often accompany trust. One such trust-enhancing activity is especially present in the German model for developing trust, which due to its reliance on standardized training and internships, focuses on keeping processes flowing due to confidence in and reliance on others' work. In contrast, less training in the United States often leads to a lack of trust and little confidence in work. Therefore, trust bridges may not as visible in the American corporate world. Political connections often have a greater impact on communities that experience very little corruption. This means that people are not relying on bribes or other forms of under the table compensation to make business and personal decisions. Also, this may partially explain research on municipalities, which found that established trust bridges led to government growth and increased profitability of firms.

Relationships that are rooted in trust discourage people from engaging in dishonest behavior. One can therefore argue that corruption inhibits the foundation of relationships. When discovered, corruption can ruin a reputation. Once trust bridges are destroyed, they are difficult to rebuild. In today's global economy that is ruled by rapid, if not constant, communication and connection through technology, global trust standards can converge where people hold each other to the same standards. This makes international business easier because it reduces the necessity of local standards, which often results in greater costs for companies since they have to meet different standards in every country of operation. If a global standard was in place, every country would more likely partake in international business interactions, and therefore would have a better chance of establishing trust bridges. In addition, companies and managers making crucial decisions based on current trust bridges need to exercise less oversight. All this translates into more effective and efficient use of resources. Thus, trust bridges not only reduce the likelihood of corruption, but also lead to more efficient and profitable business.

CHAPTER 22

Guilt or Competition: Wining the Cyber-Espionage War

Korea Times, June 2014

**Visible from space but not finding
a new purpose.**

Remindful of Emile Zola's 'J'accuse' about anti-Semitism in France, the United States has charged five officials in the Chinese People's Liberation Army of hacking into U.S. commercial computers and stealing top-secret trade information. The hackers stand accused of taking confidential nuclear and solar technology data for the benefit of their firms, thus giving Chinese businesses an unfair competitive advantage. Chinese officials have vehemently denounced these "fictitious allegations" and claim that they threaten the established mutual trust between China and the United States.

Is this just another stalemate or what is the news here? The Chinese have collected information from the United States for quite some time, just as the Russians, Germans, and French have. It is also now common knowledge that the United States gathers extensive information from China as well as Germany and many other nations. In the latter case, U.S. economic and security activity lead to a tangible disruption of United States–German relations. The German collective memory of an all-knowing and very oppressive domestic intelligence service (Stasi) in the GDR are only 25 years old. Many Germans also complained: "Spying. . .that is not what you do between friends". Is the German notion solely naïve? Why, then, is this kerfuffle taken more seriously than routine hacking?

Some speculate that this entire affair is "running a new pig through town," a European way of referring to new actions designed to move attention away from policy failures. Perhaps we are witnessing a plan designed to distract from the current criticism of Obamacare or Veterans Affairs.

Or is this Chinese incident truly more serious than regular cyber-espionage? America's displeasure seems to be based on its discovery of a linkage between security measures and industrial espionage. Security espionage benefits from an international consensus that governments have the responsibility to learn about any measures taken abroad which could endanger their own citizens. Industrial, or economic espionage however, is seen as much more unacceptable if governments intervene abroad for the sake of their businesses. The United States differentiates accordingly, and in light of the now great importance of international business, shares its view with other nations. The difference is also well expressed in a terminology, which clearly separates intelligence agents from spies.

If all this is a competitiveness issue, then of course proceeding against the hackers is not enough. Steps must also be taken against the users of the maliciously obtained information, since it is the use not just the possession, which causes the greatest damage.

Is America hypocritical in charging the Chinese with cyber-espionage?

When the United States was still a young nation and the U.K. was the world leader in innovation, America also participated in espionage (and did not pay for intellectual property) in order to advance technologically. Perhaps China will ensure its protection once it has enough of its own property to protect.

Is all this only a U.S.–Chinese problem, or is industrial espionage a key problem around the world? Does the punishment reflect a special fear of Chinese reverse engineering capabilities?

There may be a new era of knowledge acquisition and distribution where military/political insights are either linked to economic/production knowledge, or are kept separate from each other. Right now, the world trend seems to be in the direction of obtaining information in all areas of human activity, and to use it for any advance possible.

The United States can be the key bulwark separating military and business knowledge. Sanctions against five Chinese individuals will not produce any major direct curtailment of information acquisition and use. But there can be a clear symbolic effect.

This dispute over espionage is just another demonstration of the ultimate clash between the United States and China. They have different perspectives of the role of the State and business. If the sanctions bring a change in the global differentiation between types and use of information, then the actions taken against the five individuals are well worth the effort. If not, we are witnessing the erasure of another line in the sand. For the sake of an internationally level playing field and the encouragement of fair competition and market-driven activities, let us hope that this wake-up call stirs new thinking around the world.

CHAPTER 23

The European Prayer of Saint Augustine (with Ilkka A. Ronkainen)

McDonough Business, Summer 2004

The European Union grew from 15 to 25 members on May 1. For 480 million Europeans, borders should have opened for free movement of people, ideas, and commerce. But politics and politicians have sharply restrained that movement. Many in the old Europe fear disaster from a rapid influx of people. Workers from low-income nations within the expanded European Union could come to steal the few manual jobs still held precariously by locals. Immigrants may take advantage of generous health care, unemployment, or welfare systems. And they will never go home once they discover the burial benefits. The new EU members disagree. They point to a long history in which they have been occupied, exploited, and oppressed. Yet, they have never left their countries. Quite telling is the comment of a Hungarian who points out that "we live in brick houses" to explain that families have stayed in place for centuries.

Perhaps a few excursions abroad, but never a move!

Right now, fear has the political upper hand. The old European nations have implemented special escape clauses to safeguard their systems. An abundance of regulations is aimed against the new Europeans. For up to 7 years, they will need special work permits, will be restricted in their unemployment and health care benefits, and constrained in their retirement programs. The current European expansion is remindful of the prayer of Saint Augustine: "Lord make me chaste—but not yet!" There are key drawbacks to such an arrangement. Delay introduces uncertainty, discontent, and suffering. Those seeking benefits are disappointed. Their hopes of rapid improvement and dreams of equality are shattered. After a century of misery due to accidents of history and geography, here is another painful setback. It was, after all, EU proximity that enabled the new member countries to reform their economies and political systems in the short time period since the downfall of Communism. Those seeking to postpone the effects of expansion only weaken their station. Jobs will continue to move to locations where they are performed better and at a lower price. There will be no inflow of new enthusiasm and elasticity. Rather than welcoming a shift to a new productive era, there is now a stultifying wait for the "inevitable," discouraging the old but not encouraging the new.

Europe is different from the United States, but some post-World War II U.S. experience can offer insights. Each year, on average, every seventh American moves. Most moves are within the same county, or within the same state. But year after year, U.S. movers to a different state almost reach 3 percent of the population. That is the equivalent of the entire U.S. population transitioning to a new home state in little more than one generation. Not everybody moves equally. The wealthy and well-entrenched have very low migration patterns. Those with low household incomes are the most avid movers, seeking new opportunities. Young adults move frequently to broaden their views. All this mobility has maintained a sense of adventure in America. It has retained a spirit of flexibility and exploration. If there are no new jobs in Illinois but lots of new opportunities in Arizona, then that is where many people go. There has been the creation of entirely new regional industry and service clusters.

There remains strong local pride of place yet there is little xenophobic fear from out-of-state migrants. Vermonters do not fear Virginians! What does all this me mean for the new Europe? The opportunities to pick up and move are there, and those ready to move would fill a vital need. The decline in fertility and aging of the population will reduce the workforce by 5.5 percent by the year 2020 in the old EU. Even large increases in mobility would only represent a small population flow (which is now less than one half of one percent). People deserve to explore new options. New moves may well become an action signal for the European economy and way of thinking. This is a key opportunity to enrich the quality of life of regions and individuals. A long-term view is necessary. Migration may not result in permanent relocation. Individuals who go back home stimulate investment by setting up businesses and employing others. Many immigrants, rather than looking for a handout, want to develop their own base: home ownership, better educational opportunities, as well as health and economic security. All these moves will change cultures. After all, culture is the result of learned behavior and adjustment to new conditions. Opening up to others should bring the reward of growing flexibility, better understanding, and rising tolerance levels. Mobility has brought the power of improvisation and adjustment to the United States. Today's world needs a Europe of courage, innovation and a willingness to take risks, with citizens that want new members to be part of, rather than apart, from them. It is time for traditionalists to discard the remaining barriers to mobility and to embrace with pride and happiness the new Europeans.

SECTION IV

Our Daily Lives with a Global Perspective

CHAPTER 24

International Health Care of the Future: The Evolving Doctor (with Anna Astvatsatryan)

Sri Lanka Guardian, October 2014

Getting inoculated sometimes hurts a bit.

Is it possible to make high-quality medical care affordable to everyone? Finding the "golden mean" in health care is a hot topic of discussion. Patients and governments both agree that health care needs to be effective, accessible, and affordable. The search for a balance pushes advocacy groups to seek unconventional solutions. New technologies may offer easier access to providers and allow medical experts to review patient complaints. Globalization is said to open doors to geographically more diverse and therefore less expensive treatment options. Can new technologies in new places really make a difference in the field?

Patients often find their own solutions. International medical tourism, where patients travel to low-cost medical locations, to take advantage of cheaper health care services, has grown exponentially. Many countries such as Israel specialize in certain treatments; others emphasize their low costs of health care across the board. According to "Patients Beyond Borders," an international medical tourism association, Brazil, Costa, Rica, and India are among the top medical tourism destinations. The top specialties for medical travelers include cosmetic surgery, dentistry, and cardiovascular surgeries such as angioplasty and transplants.

Researchers and advocates in the United States are looking for solutions to keep their patients inside the local medical care market by offering alternative medical treatments. The Washington Post reports about a study by Professor Rashid Bashrur of the University of Michigan that focuses on telemedicine—virtual medical care when doctors study and advise their patients remotely. This study shows that telemedicine, the use of medical information exchanged from one site to another does matter. It can reduce the length of hospital stays and numbers of emergency visits, and provide remote connection between doctor and patient. Telemedicine technology can reduce the health care costs for patients and increase the speed of conversation between patients and medical experts. Yet increased virtual medical care can also lead to more frequent appointments with nurses. In an international context, virtual healthcare may be used as an alternative to medical tourism. The main considerations are language and communications barriers that can occur between doctors and patients. Lack of communication will not play a big role if the patient is a child, but may cause trouble with older generations.

New automation technology will convert a growing number of health care providers into technical experts. That tendency is quite visible in orthopedics, where large efforts and resources go into the development of prosthetics. In 2006, the Defense Advanced Research Projects Agency, part of the Defense Department, launched a $120 million prosthetics program. Another aspect is the effectiveness of the new technology where analysis of large volumes of data will provide new research tools for the medical experts. Such an approach may, however, exclude much of the "human factor" from health care. Another issue is the pricing for such kind of "technological" medical care. What should be the price difference between an actual doctor and nurse and a beeping computer?

New technology can also make medical treatment more holistic. Currently, after a diagnosis and a prescription, doctors typically do not have much control over a patient's behavior. It is up to the patients to decide to take the prescribed medicine on time and in the suggested dosage or not take it at all. The use of automated systems can control the treatment process. Companies such as EvaStarMedical, Cytta, and Microchips, which I advise and in which I hold stocks, are very promising firms. They have begun implanting chips with drug reservoirs in patients. These chips can be implanted directly under the skin, delivering doses of pharmaceuticals or birth control hormones at the same time each day. The implanted chip is designed to be remote-controlled and governed by medical professionals whose expertise is in technology rather than medicine. This technology will help older patients that tend to forget to take their medicine. It will also decrease the workload for many health care providers. Is it necessarily a good thing? It may disemploy some physicians, but can also be viewed as a fundamental industrial change. Gutenberg's invention of the printing press is a great example of technological progress and its consequences, when a new and effective technology of printing basically left monks and other document copiers jobless. On the other hand, new medical technology will eliminate a great deal of person-to-person communications. Most of the patients, especially the older folks, need and value good bedside manners. Research has shown that patients who feel that their provider has good bedside manner are more compliant with treatment regimens, have more positive health outcomes, and are more satisfied with the care that they receive.

The main question remains if patients actually want to save money on health care in exchange for a medical system with minimal interpersonal communication and very limited face-to-face meetings. Are patients ready for a medical system where the doctor knows all about them but still very little of them?

CHAPTER 25

Super Bowl Versus Olympics: Discerning the Marketing Differences (with Charles J. Skuba)

Japan Today, January 2014

Although the Super Bowl does reach viewers around the world, Olympic advertisers will be communicating with a much broader audience from diverse cultures who will bring with them a different set of interests and emotions. To persuade such a multicultural audience, advertising will need to seek commonalities of the mind and heart.

Global advertising agencies have the expertise to create messages that work across borders and avoid the danger of leaving broad groups of viewers bewildered or, worse, offended. We offer five winning techniques (not exclusive to each other) for creative messaging to global audiences during the Olympics in national and global media campaigns.

The best brands inspire and capture positive, if not joyful, emotion in their customers. Marketers know that emotion often trumps reason in purchase decisions. Dig deep into any customer psyche, whether of a business decision maker or a teenage gamer, and you will find a bundle of emotions that are common to people across cultures. Although there are cultural differences in what stirs emotion, some things are universal, like love stories and the pursuit of dreams. For the 2012 London Olympic Games, P&G launched the global "Thank You Mom" campaign that celebrated the love of young Olympic athletes and their mothers. There may be no more powerful bond than the love between a mom and her child and that love is a universal emotion. Whenever we show the campaign film in class, it is guaranteed to start tears flowing. And, P&G's "Thank You Mom app" that allows people to thank their own moms crosses cultural boundaries. The film industry has conditioned viewers across the world to crave dramatic, expansive imagery. The most successful global films create a powerful impact in sight and sound. The Avengers amaze and inspire audiences globally with their technological and artistic power. The Olympics are a key opportunity for grand imagery.

Marketers regularly use striking visuals to capture attention but the bar is being raised. A dramatic recent marketing event was the Red Bull Stratos mission and the awe-inspiring free fall jump of Felix Baumgartner from his stratospheric balloon. Millions of people around the world have seen the video and Red Bull continues to reap global benefits from the event. Inspiring sounds and music hand-in-hand with expansive imagery are sounds and music. Music enhances visuals for dramatic and emotional impact. Marketers must be careful with music selection. Coca-Cola has long used "happiness" music to appeal to young people around the world. Coca-Cola's use of music and visuals in David Corey's "The World of Ours" song for the 2014 FIFA World Cup in Brazil builds from the joyful 2010 campaign song, K'Naaan's "Wavin' Flag." Naturally, if the music is great, people will want to share it. Coca-Cola, Facebook, and Spotify created a partnership to allow people around the world with access to Coca-Cola's campaign music.

If you want simple communication of an idea, it is hard to beat symbolism. IBM employs symbolism to enhance and distinguish its campaign and product messaging in its "Smarter Planet." If you can show product advantage in advertising, it is hardworking marketing. The trick is to get people's attention to your message. Samsung built in product demonstration for its Galaxy SII throughout its London 2012 Olympics advertising after getting attention through David Beckham's wringing a gong with a well-placed kick. Also, marketers would be smart to walk away from messaging that depends upon slang or references to national pop culture. If you did not grow up watching American television, you might not get a lot of pop culture references that U.S. audiences instantly understand. The advertising that audiences will see during the upcoming Super Bowl will be uniquely tuned to American audiences while that of the Olympics will be globally focused. We are confident that both will employ many of the techniques identified here. Marketers are literally going for the global gold. For the audience, the Olympic marketing messages will be quite different from the ones of the Super Bowl but well worth waiting for.

CHAPTER 26

Is It Just Me?

Korea Times, October 2010

Going for the new and unknown is my job. I am a university professor and do my professing through research, teaching, and writing. Most of my activities tend to be new. I never really know how a class discussion will turn out. When formulating research hypothesis, the whole idea is to be wide open to new indications and findings. And even in the 10th edition of my text book, there are major new directions and changes to be captured.

Yet, thinking new or unexpected thoughts is disquieting to some. For example, I still dream of living some day in a castle. To many friends and neighbors, this is one of those silly dreams which should have been shed decades ago. Sometimes, when I describe my castle, people even get openly hostile, declaring such thoughts to be outlandish, wasteful and reflective of delusions of grandeur. They tell me that spending even a minute on such ideas takes away from productivity and is a giant waste. But I have discovered that I may not be alone.

On occasions when I mention castles, I see eyes light up, reflecting dreams remembered and imagination recaptured. The voices might be slightly lowered, but the intensity of the conversation picks up. Sometimes we even repair to the Internet and do some searches. Entering, for example, "Schloss Verkauf" under Google brings up the hunting castle in Magdeburg, the castle with the moat near Berlin, the family castle from the 16th century in Bavaria. There are many more in Austria, Switzerland, France, and Italy. Some of them come with an ante-castle area of large proportion. Many have the requisite tower, the horse stables, and the huge gate. Then there are those with bordering forest areas or vineyards. Some are fully restored, others need some help, but they all require loving tender care—if only because preservation regulations require it. The price typically seems reasonable or even low when compared to real estate prices in many of the metropolis. I am told about the deleterious effects of a castle. There are the terrible tax burdens, the upkeep and maintenance nightmares, the isolation, and the total excess of space.

Forests may mean that one has to pay for a forester. Woods will have to be scouted regularly for infested trees. The deer population will have to be managed. Who shovels the snow in winter? All, so true. But then I think of my youth, when dreaming about special things was not out of reach, but rather part and parcel of life. Over time, not too many dreams of childhood have been preserved. Yet, the move to a castle is not an introverted return to the olden days, but in its own way a new, pioneering action. A new environment, an entirely different set of challenges, new neighbors, combined with history and closeness to nature. It is also a new perspective. Castles, by their very nature, tend to have a far-reaching outlook. Typically, they are built on top of a hill or even a mountain, with the tower reaching well above the trees. After all, you want to see who is coming up the road.

Just as the climbing of a mountain lets you see vistas never taken in before, a castle gives an overview. A castle reflects promises of safety and freedom. There is an aura of peace and a welcoming of guests. A certain ampleness is also built into castles. There is the knights room, the salon, the dining hall, and of course, the ballroom. What a feeling of open space! As time flies by, in many societies one is encouraged to settle down, which means to settle for what we have. Contentment eliminates pain. But it also pours concrete onto our limitations and focuses us on the low end of the horizon. By contrast, sleep research tells us that dreams help sustain life. Perhaps even God was dreaming when he did his creating. Castles are not easy. Even the Bavarian King Ludwig, who built Neuschwanstein, the model for later replicas by Disney, learned that harsh reality. When he built too many castles, he was deposed, and, some say murdered. I think that we all need our castles. We are all born with some, we drop them often, but there is a time to have our dreams return. A castle can be our defiance of time, our dedication to life and culture. You do not have to be a king to dream, but if you get your castle, you will be a king.

CHAPTER 27

Royal Wedding
(with Mariele Marki)

Korea Times, February 2011

Ludwig King is not quite the same
as King Ludwig.

On Friday, the royal wedding of Prince William of England and Kate Middleton took place. Hundreds of millions of viewers around the world had their eyes glued to television units transmitting the momentous event. If student action at Georgetown University is an indicator, in the United States at three in the morning, many Americans tuned into live coverage of the royal wedding. Most major media networks were broadcasting from London.

According to a study by Nielsen, a leader in market research, "United States news and media outlets have out-published their U.K. counterparts in terms of wedding coverage." The fascination and romanticism that the

United States has for the royal family and the increase in attention ever since the engagement was announced last November, demonstrates the strong ties between the United States and the United Kingdom. This cultural connection is an excellent example of a concept developed in international business. Psychological distance is the perceived distance from a firm to a foreign market, caused by cultural variables, legal factors, history and other societal norms.

A common model used to demonstrate this theory is a comparison of the link between the United States and Canada, and the United States and Mexico. Americans tend to identify more with Canada than with Mexico. Both countries border the United States, but for reasons of language and culture, Canada appears to be psychologically much closer. While the United States and the United Kingdom share the same language and have a linked history, one can also see the allure of royalty in both cultures. Disney princesses have a strong presence in every young girl's child-hood in the United States and many movies center around the plot of a fairytale with the prince and princess living happily ever after. Women want to be treated like princesses and it is culturally very common to rejoice when one has "found her prince." Even though the United States has not had a royal leader in centuries, news on royal families is a regular part of television and magazine entertainment. A large portion of the American population maintains a high level of interest in all that is regal. Psychological proximity is much preferable to psychological distance. It helps business, creates friendships, and leads to national decisions which are often unabashedly in favor of one's friends. Psychological distance in turn tends to slow down relationships and, in a proverb mentioned by international travelers, affects the quality of the water one might other-wise share. That makes it important that all nations work on bridging distances through collaboration, mutual visits, and confidence-building measures.

Every business transaction is another step in mutual diplomacy which links nations together. Some nations even built their growth and success based on tying the knot and closing the distance. For example, for cen-turies, the proverb in Europe was "Tu Felix Austria, nube," meaning that (in order to prosper), you, lucky Austria, just get married. However, as international business theory shows us, the best quality of psychological proximity occurs when it is close but not too close. Closeness creates better relationships and does make it easier for firms to enter markets. But too much of a focus on similarities can lead to what may be considered unwelcome intrusiveness, and lets managers lose sight of important differences. Even between the United States and the United Kingdom, there are behavioral and language differences which are ignored at great peril. Just think of how new acquaintances address each other or how one talks about past accomplishments. The fact that England still has a royal family and a society quite different from the United States makes the wedding interesting. But interest does not mean that Americans would want to have royalty at home. Actually, many Americans would quite resent attempts to crown a domestic king. But that is discussed best over a pot of tea.

CHAPTER 28

What We Should Be Teaching Kids That Is Not Found in Heavy Books (with Thomas Czinkota)

Shanghai Daily, November 2009

Devastating impression : A home without books.

There is no doubt that children today are being overworked and over-scheduled—but do the Czinkota brothers have a good point about what education should be? We just concluded the fall school vacation. Between us two brothers, we have three children, 6, 7, and 10, with whom we spent the week in conversation, playing, and thinking.

Here are some of the issues that we considered, but are not sure that we solved: Are children overworked? Over time growing societal surpluses have made it possible to enjoy the fruits of our labors. We no longer learn only because we have to, but because we want to and we can focus on learning about history and enjoyment of art, music and poetry, about beauty. Even though the need for learning has changed, the process and conditions of learning have not been altered to provide for a more relaxed childhood. Kids are increasingly over-scheduled little beasts of burden with more work of greater complexity carried in ever heavier knapsacks on wheels. The available knowledge has increased greatly. Yet, our children keep on learning the way their parents did. Are we perhaps maintaining an outdated approach, applying it to vastly increased quantities of content with a greatly diminished half-life? Memory outdated? Could it be that all we are doing is cramming our children's brains with more useless stuff?

We exert pressure on our children so that they learn. Just as high pressure can transform coal into diamonds, perhaps our children grow more talented. We punish them for not doing sufficient work. Boredom is no excuse. Of course, shouldn't we ask why the same child is not getting bored by TV shows, discussions with friends, or playing with dolls? In a pharmacological society, many kids are given prescription pills to cure what once was seen as typical (highly active) child behavior. We have even seen children who have their own personal assistant charged with keeping them focused. But there are also procedural learning questions: Why do children still memorize? Memorization had its origins when there was no print, no dictionaries, and therefore no institutional retention. Priests and monks had to memorize in order to pass on society's knowledge—they were the living word.

Today, we have Google, Bing, Wikipedia; all systems that remember things for us. Of course, it is said that by subscribing to Wikipedia we are buying into the hidden agenda of secretive editors. Well, why not? For centuries we have bought into the hidden agendas of the secretive editors of the Oxford Dictionary. Even the monks and scribes who laboriously produced manuscripts, added or eliminated details. So the flexibility and adjustment of materials has a long tradition. How much knowledge does a child realistically need? Will (or should) the acquired knowledge ever be useful for anything? Does it make sense to dispense knowledge in a shotgun approach (we give you everything and hope some of it helps)? There is always a great reluctance to move away from existing patterns.

There used to be a firm conviction that only the slide rule would maintain the algebraic memories of children. After our vacation together, we ask ourselves whether it is not much more important to spend time with our children to play more, listen to and perform more music, exercise in more sports, engage in more theater productions. We need to explain to them the things they need to know—for example about morals, values, a sense of excitement, and pleasure; about the facts of life, that prices are typically not the result of costs but of demand and supply; about friendship, and the enjoyment and benefits of new people networks. With such knowledge, our children might not be able to avoid a global trade and financial crisis, but at least they will understand it and react to it.

CHAPTER 29

Assault at the Cathedral

Egypt News, January 2016

When we go to church to pray for rain, we
should carry an umbrella.

On New Year's Eve, there were mass attacks on women in Cologne, Germany. More than a thousand young men, many of them with an apparent migration background, congregated next to the famous cathedral of Cologne where they assaulted, groped, and even raped women passing by. Local police, far outnumbered, did not intervene in the mayhem. In the days to follow, police, press, and government tried to downplay the disaster, in order to avoid controversy about migrants, of which Germany admitted more than one million in 2015, with many more to come.

Since then, statements by police who had been ordered to stand down, by eye witnesses and by social media, have emboldened the victims to file more than 625 criminal complaints with 40 percent of them related to sexual assault. Many of the alleged attackers are Arab or North

African, which has led to severe discontent with the government and its migration policy. There have been a series of protests, particularly in eastern Germany, blaming Chancellor Angela Merkel's government and her open-door refugee policies.

Beyond the very serious criminal charges which are for the police and judiciary to resolve three additional serious questions. First, are European countries such as Germany ready to accept so many refugees both mentally and physically? Second, given the huge number of migrants still in motion, who will provide them with a domicile? Third, and most importantly, the desire for temporary tranquility has invalidated the fight for the equality of women, shod the aversion of violence against women, and done so at a dangerous cost to societal transparency and progress.

For decades, even centuries, Western countries have been trading partners with authoritarian regimes in the Middle East, selling weapons, automobiles, and other lucrative products. But the encouragement of an Arab Spring has led mainly to an Arab Fall. Yet, a large financial overhang, mainly resulting from international business, has not led to an assimilation of values and behavior. Instead many funds are used to help the distribution of fierce rhetoric, giving rise to Osama Bin Laden and many other extremists. These developments are paired with an asymmetry of political correctness in the Western World, leading to new rope which the victim sells to its miscreant.

With decreasing demands for mutual integration, concurrently rising migration and outdistanced procreation, there are fewer viable landing strips for students, women, and willing economic participants.

Right now, many of the migrants seek out primarily Germany and Sweden as asylum territories, which is understandable in light of the accommodations and benefits offered. But there are also important cultural milestones and preferences of governments and citizens who receive the human wave. Integration means that hosts learn more about their visitors, but also requires the new arrivals to accept key standards and expectations of their hosts. Although large immigration is likely to dilute rigid norms, it also must lead to asymptotic movement toward established standards.

The EU, taking on a leadership role consistent with the Treaty of Lisbon, should protect the human rights of asylum seekers, but also has right to determine where this protection should take place. For example, the Middle East and Africa have many locations where refugees can be housed, fed and clothed, and protected. Countries such as China and India could develop entire settlement policies for the resolution of a global problem. These are not meant to create new colonies, but rather endorse the establishment of pop-up protectorates, to temporarily provide succor, shelter, and peace to refugees.

Third, and perhaps most chillingly because it can set the future rails for disaster, is the failure of the public media to distribute honest information rapidly. An almost week-long delay of media reports was broken only when too many other sources broke the mantra of keeping bad news about migrants out of the public spotlight. This is wrong! Silence is a blow to the victims of violence, and lets them be hunted like game. Women deserve better.

The violent, brutal, and sexist treatment of women must be combated radically. The event in Cologne reveals a major flaw societal shortcoming which cannot be tolerated. Germany is an internationalized country due to the composition of its population and its dependence on foreign trade. If it wishes to continue with its international leadership role, Germany must recognize that such role is one of immersion into the world which must result in simultaneous juridical, social, and economic leadership. Female equality is a crucial entitlement for more than half of the population. To declare otherwise is wrong for the native locals as well for the wave of newly arriving migrants. The events in Cologne must not become the opening act for continued misery and disrepute.

The attempt to muffle the powerless laments of the victims with the blanket of public silence is most treacherous. One should not cry "fire" in a cinema, but doing so is encouraged when the flames are in the roof. The self-motivated absconders must recognize how their behavior has fertilized the ground for future misinformation and knowledge abuse. Effective steps must be taken to truly make a difference. It is time for such action with specific details clearly spelled out by democratic transparency. As was already promulgated by St. John: "And you will know the truth and the truth will make you free."

CHAPTER 30

Why the Tranatlantic Trade and Investment Partnership Is More Important Than TPP (with Valbona Zeneli)

The Diplomat, January 2016

Private financial flows vastly outperform trade flows 100:1

The Trans-Pacific Partnership (TPP) is a planned free trade agreement covering 12 countries from North and South America to the Pacific Rim. The Trans-Atlantic Trade and Investment Partnership (TTIP) is a planned free trade agreement between the United States and the European Union.

Both represent the main trade negotiation motions of the current global economic system.

The TPP negotiations were successfully concluded in October 2015 after 4 years of intensive talks. Legislative ratification will be the next step. TTIP has been under negotiation since June 2013; some hopes are for completion by the end of 2016. Both are unlikely to be ratified in their current form under the Trump's Administration. The combined trans-Pacific and trans-Atlantic space covered by the two new agreements makes up 60.33 percent of the world economy, and 22 percent of its population, according to data compiled by the International Monetary Fund.

The two agreements are very similar in terms of market shares and populations, but they differ in terms of per capita incomes and living standards. According to International Monetary Fund data, the TPP economies represent 27.3 percent of the world's purchasing power parity, measured through its gross domestic product (GDP), and 10.7 percent of the world's population. The TTIP economies represent 33 percent of the world GDP, with 11.2 percent of the population. The average per capita GDP for the 12 TPP countries is $ 30,697, whereas the TTIP average income is $47,607. Beyond the differences in membership; however, there are also notable differences in the scope and goals of the agreements themselves. First, TPP is focused at opening markets and eliminating tariff barriers on trade and investment, whereas TTIP is mainly focused on foreign direct investment (FDI).

Since the year 2000, U.S. investment in the European economic area has made up 55 percent of the total U.S. outward (FDI), compared to 21 percent in the TPP economy, and only 1.4 percent in the Chinese economy. Similarly, the European Union's FDI in the United States comes to 61 percent, in comparison to 24 percent from the 11 countries included in the TPP.

Trans-Atlantic tariffs on average are much lower than the trans-Pacific ones, with an average of only 4 percent trade tariffs across the Atlantic. Exceptions are a few highly regulated sectors such as textiles and the agriculture and automobile industry. TTIP negotiations aim at improving the regulatory convergence to facilitate trade and investments, reducing the nontariff barriers, and opening up the service market across the Atlantic.

Second, TTIP is more ambitious in comparison to TTP. In addition to its financial and economic benefits, TTIP will have a larger geostrategic impact, since it vicariously reinforces the strong ties that exist between Europe and the United States. TTIP is a natural Western partnership, with mature, well-developed and consolidated markets, on the one hand, and a strong defense relationship based on the North Atlantic Treaty Organization (NATO) on the other hand. Both components are missing in Asia. Those strategic realities, as well as economic ones, mean the TTIP will have more lasting importance than the TPP. For one thing, the trans-Atlantic economy is the innovation powerhouse of the global economy, and a crucial element in future growth and development. The United States is the largest global spender on R&D, as a single economy, reprising its role as the dominant force in global research across numerous industries. It spent almost 3 percent of its GDP on R&D in 2014, more than $465 billion, making up 32 percent of the share of global R&D spending. The European Union combined spends on average a little more than 2 percent of its GDP (or $283 billion), a little more than 20 percent of the world's total. Germany is the biggest spender in the European Union, with almost 3 percent of its GDP.

Technology is the key driver of development, and differences among regions in R&D economies are narrowing. China's R&D spending has been increasing quickly over the last 10 years, as it wants to evolve from a manufacturing-centric model—making products designed and developed in the West—to an innovation-based consumer economy. Spending 2 percent of the GDP, it makes up 17.5 percent of the world's total R&D spending, but it might surpass the United States if it reaches its target of 3 percent by 2020. Given the size and scope of the trans-Atlantic economy, standards negotiated by the United States and the EU could become a benchmark for future global rules, inhibiting the emergence and acceptance of competing standards. Arguably, TTIP will be the West's last best opportunity to set global rules as the emerging markets continue to gain ground.

The deal reached last December at the UN Climate Summit to reduce global greenhouse gas emissions showed that the EU and the United States then contained the political will and the resources to set the standards. In fact, TTIP's sustainable energy framework chapter would offer both political and economic impetus to both sides of the Atlantic. It goes without saying that TTIP and TPP are strategically interlinked with each other. Both agreements are important in terms of how the trans-Atlantic partners jointly best relate to newly rising powers, and whether the West will set the new standards of the international economic order. Both TTIP and TPP take on an increasing strategic importance in light of the continuously growing role of China, and other emerging markets in the global economy. Moreover, there may be insufficient content for change to re-balance inequities between the nations.

Achieving progress in the simplification of trade and investment relations in the framework of the two negotiated agreements TTIP and TPP, which make up more than 60 percent of the world economy, would allow the World Trade Organization (WTO) to expand its useful life. TPP's conclusion is important. Higher growth rates in the United States will help the European economy through increased exports, but TPP also needs to reinforce the geopolitical reality of rebalancing toward Asia. More pressure on Europe to engage in TTIP may help to shape and benefit from the free trade deals. Despite all difficulties and objections (internal and external), achieving progress in the simplification of trade and investment relations is important to global prosperity. The approaches taken by TTP and TTIP are the future of trade negotiations—tightly focused talks between selected participants aiming for specific improvements in fields of their trading or investment advantage by becoming better at growingly, making, planning or coordinating outcomes. Operating within such framework can generate mutual and equitable benefits and can also assist in the future of the WTO.

CHAPTER 31

The World Trade Organization (WTO): Challenges and Solution (with Valbona Zeneli)

February 2016

The GATT and WTO have written the rule book for trade and investment around ithe world.

The World Trade Organization (WTO) and its predecessor, the General Agreement on Tariffs and Trade (GATT) has been one of the most successful international institutions. But besides its positive effects, the WTO's framework has also brought some sense of discomfort, fear, and painful economic adjustment to meet international competition. Even at its peak surrounding the Uruguay Round (1986 to 1994), the question arose whether the WTO could effectively handle broader social issues. Pollution, global warming, diseases, and structural unemployment were possible macroeconomic factors seeking inclusion into the WTO framework. None of these issues have been effectively addressed, much less solved, by the WTO.

The Doha Round of negotiations started in November 2001 aiming at achieving major reforms in the international trading system with an explicit focus on developing countries. It has failed and still remains incomplete until this day. Major obstacles still remain over several key issues such as agricultural sectors, free trade of services, and intellectual property rights. The number of WTO members has grown from 27 in 1948, and 123 nations in 1994 to 162 and has made the system unwieldy. The continuation of the unanimous voting requirement for progress and agreement has brought a slow and squealing forward motion to a standstill.

It is not surprising that, in the light of pervasive terror threats, politicians tend to focus on the high-intensity politics of national security and war, as opposed to the low-intensity politics of trade and investment.

The global recession only intensified this tendency to ignore international economic issues, as attention shifted to domestic job creation, security, and protection of domestic credit markets.

In consequence to continued stalemates and disagreements in the Doha round, it appears that liberalization has taken a new approach outside the WTO. The last two decades have led to a do-it-yourself approach, defined by mega-regional agreements and preferential plurilateral trade negotiations, handmade for only a limited number of players. According to WTO data, as of December 2015, there are 619 Regional Trade Agreements (RTAs) under negotiation globally, with 265 of those currently in force. Such agreements rest on the ambition to further liberalize and promote a global 21st century by selectively addressing trade and investment barriers. A number of the topics discussed are similar to those not finalized by previous multilateral talks. The Trans-Pacific Partnership (TPP) and the Trans-Atlantic Trade and Investment Partnership (TTIP) are two major new trade agreements which may shore up the international trade system.

Solutions

With baby boomers retiring and millennials starting to staff today's corporations, there is remarkable cultural change and challenge within organizations, which exert effect on the political structures of the next decade, including trade and the WTO.

The last 20 years have given fertile ground to criticism regarding the WTO, particularly to claims that the organization has reached its limit of complexity. Some suggest that future negotiations might be conducted as individual initiatives with limited objectives, as opposed to large negotiation rounds that aim to accomplish numerous goals simultaneously. Successful implementation of a "plurilateral plus model" could eventually create a higher equilibrium by extending the benefit of regional and bilateral agreements to all WTO members, even if the obligations would bind only the initial members of the agreements and others as they join it.

On the other side, the WTO system does not operate in isolation of other international trade policy. Liberalization coming by other means (unilaterally and bilaterally) is likely to push for further liberalization at the WTO negotiations too. Similarly, the Uruguay Round was knocked *on* track because North America signed the NAFTA agreement and Europe created its single market. The fear factor is important. Fear of missing out on new benefits concentrate political minds.

It may also be possible to introduce new groups of countries in the WTO, and having their negotiation concentrated on one of four key areas: to grow, to make, to create economic activity, or to coordinate economic activity. That should make decisions more pertinent and rapid. The WTO also broadens its reach, including nongovernmental organizations and other political actors.

Finally, the WTO could help implement activities that support social causes. Many other organizations, such as the International Labor Organization and the World Bank, already focus on issues surrounding socioeconomic development. The WTO should play a supportive, but not a primary role in these issues. For example, the International Trade Centre, co-sponsored by UNCTAD/GATT, could provide training on how to commercialize rain forests without causing excessive damage to the environment or communities within them.

The core contribution of the WTO, however, will be in the fact that the flag follows trade and investment. Over time, increased economic ties will cross-pollinate cultures, values, and ethics between economic partners and, together with the income effects on individuals and countries, cause changes in the social arena, which need to be supported in their impact.

CHAPTER 32

Does the WTO Contribute to World Trade? (with Valbona Zeneli)

February 2016

Too much of a good thing can cause friction.

In 1948, after years of negotiations, more than 50 nations signed the Havana Charter to create the International Trade Organization (ITO). But in the 1950s, President Truman decided not to resubmit the ITO charter to Congress for ratification, due to perceived threats to national sovereignty and the danger of too much ITO intervention in markets. The result was the much more limited General Agreement on Tariffs and Trade (GATT), which brought rules and regulations to world trade. A major breakthrough occurred in 1994. Negotiators launched a totally new organization, which the Uruguay Round (1986 to 1994) negotiations agreed on—the World Trade Organization (WTO).

After two politically and economically charged decades, we find that the WTO has been one of the most successful international institutions. With a rejuvenated framework of multilateralism enabled by global political shifts brought on by the fall of communism, the WTO now seeks to reduce tariffs, eliminate trade barriers and quotas, and expand coverage of services, intellectual property, foreign direct investment, and agriculture.

The WTO has encouraged international trade to prosper by fostering openness and lowering trade barriers, increasing confidence and encouraging fair trade practices. WTO rules have helped countries develop by increasing international confidence and cooperation in the system. Although there are no WTO black helicopters for enforcement, its dispute settlement process had advanced progress.

Since 1948, world trade has grown very rapidly, with trade in goods growing yearly by an average of 6 percent a year in real terms. In 1948, total world trade was valued at just above $58 billion, with the United States accounting for 34 percent of free world trade flows. Japan's imports exceeded U.S. exports by 160 percent. By 1994, world trade exceeded $4 trillion and the United States had a share of 12 percent. Almost 20 years later, in 2015, total world trade in goods and services amounted to $23 trillion. The United States held a share of 19 percent at $3,848 billion, heavily influenced by a high level of imports. Germany's share was 13 percent and Japan's $1,547 billion represented a share of 7 percent. The United States (3), the European Union (1), and China (2) have been the three largest global players in international trade since 2004 when China passed Japan.

This new international trading system has provided more choices of products and qualities for the consumers, raised incomes internationally, has stimulated economic growth, increased standards of livings. The trade system promoted by WTO has also helped promote peace and encouraged good governance. Economies that have been more open to embrace the international trade and investment policies have grown quicker than the more closed economies. Higher interdependence has allowed countries to specialize in areas where they can be more competitive using their best advantages and opportunities.

The multilateral system has produced new energy, growth, rising incomes, and better standards of living throughout the world, both in developed and developing countries. China is a perfect example of developing countries that have benefited greatly from liberalization of global trade and investment. 600 million people have been lifted out of poverty in only 30 years only, and moved up from a poor country with less than $400 per capita (on a purchasing power parity basis) in 1980, to a middle-income country in 2015 with $13,801.

China's accession to WTO in December 2001 paved the way for its economic rise and significantly contributed to increasing world trade. Two decades ago, China was only entering the playing field of international trade; in 2015, China dominates trade after an unprecedented growth spurt. In the last decades, China's growth has seen an exponential rise, with its Gross Domestic Product representing only 7.4 percent of the global economy in 2000, and almost 17 percent of it in 2015.

Tax inversions and other cross-border expansion of manufacturing chains and free trade zones have further globalized corporations. The predominance of both the English language and the U.S. dollar as global reserve currency has kept this process energetic and unifying. All this has reduced the psychic abyss of 20 years ago into a pre-Alpine hillside, supported by standardized and affordable communications.

The WTO's unenviable position over the last two decades is similar to a team trying to score on a field that was constantly changing in size, with the teams and positions frequently becoming newly named and defined, and the sports equipment taking on different weights and shapes.

The hopes for an ambitious multilateral trade deal at the WTO level have diminished, and the stalemates of the Doha round have forced countries to pursue Regional Trade Agreements. Services and agriculture remain tough to resolve. Also, the marginal benefit from additional resolutions seems less in the Doha Round, as all the "low-hanging fruits" have already been picked. According to Ambassador Moore, former Director General of the WTO, multilateralism has yet a chance to triumph. It will take some of the newcomers and participants who have only recently found their voice and power, specifically African countries and India, to come to an agreement, before other nations can get much accomplished.

CHAPTER 33

A Moral Dilemma: Understand the Challenges of Sourcing from the International Market (with Charles Skuba)

Marketing Management, Fall 2012

Distance is not dead. Goods still have to get there.

The size and scope of global corporations in the 21st century is enormous. Global corporations have vast reach and economic power, almost akin to creators and financiers like the banking dynasty of the Fugger family in the 16th century or the trade dominating East India Company of the 18th century. For example, the Coca-Cola Company sells it branded products in more than 200 countries, and Procter & Gamble estimates that 4 billion of the world's 7 billion people buy P&G brands in 180 countries every year. A recent Georgetown University study showed that if one were to equate the annual revenues of the largest global corporations with the size of the world's leading economies, many firms would rank among the top economic powers. Wal-Mart Stores, with 2010 revenues of approximately $422 billion, would rank as the 23rd largest economy in the world—ahead of countries such as Norway and Venezuela. Royal Dutch Shell would rank 26th ahead of Austria, Saudi Arabia, Argentina, and South Africa. Exxon Mobil would rank 31st ahead of Iran, Thailand, and Denmark. BP would rank 35th ahead of Greece.

This analysis also revealed that 45 companies would be listed among the top 100 economies. Of course, the balance of power within a national territory tends to come out on the side of the government: In a neck-and-neck contest, national sovereignty typically wins. This is mainly the case when it comes to the "big picture" of whether or not a country should recognize Cuba and if certain merchandise should be subject to embargoes or sanctions. The small issues, such as whether our products should be adapted to a new market abroad and at what price, tend to be overwhelmingly decided by corporations. Therefore, at this micro level, companies exert major power. Greater economic power brings "noblesse oblige," which refers to greater responsibilities and obligations regarding corporate governance, responsibility, and ethics. Many stakeholders want to know more detail on those countries with which they are spending their money. Small groups, and even individuals, track corporate behavior through the press, social media, and even webcams. Therefore, companies do not have impunity in the global economy.

They can be held accountable by customers, peers, or their host governments based on rules that can unilaterally be set in territories where their firms operate. Society determines its own level of trust in believing whether business will perform for a greater good. In cases of dissent, brand equity that has been built up laboriously over decades can be substantially damaged or even erased when corporate actions lead to significant erosion in consumer confidence. To forestall such decay, international marketers should voluntarily develop and adhere to a corporate social responsibility that demonstrates their leadership for societal needs and interests. For example, since the financial crisis and recession of 2008 to 2009, governments and public audiences have resented and even been angered by risky activities and insufficiently justified compensation levels in the financial services industry—particularly when the subsequent outcome has been very detrimental for firms and individuals caught as bystanders in the crossfire. The consequences for the industry have been major.

The Edelman Trust Barometer 2012 Annual Global Study ranked banks and financial services companies at the bottom of industries likely to "do what is right." Such negative perceptions and attitudes can easily become instrumental in the shaping of more onerous tax burdens, greater supervision by governments, and harsher penalties for the violation of rules. By contrast, at the time of the reputational descent of the financial sector, consumers around the world place a great deal of trust in technology companies, as well as companies in the automotive, food and beverages, consumer packaged goods, and telecommunications industries. Due to their substantial consideration of the consumer, and their careful considerations of collateral implications of their actions, firms in these industries tend to enjoy more freedom of action, leeway for innovation and support for expansion by both governments and consumers. Much of the preferential flexibility offered to these firms appears to be the result of being more trusted by consumers. Yet marketing-oriented companies are also subject to public scrutiny of their practices, even in areas such as production processes and labor conditions.

Resting on one's laurels typically would not work, since trust levels have to be earned anew every day. Even though one can draw from a storehouse of goodwill that has been filled over time, new actions lead to new expectations—which, in turn, may well lead to newly structured rules of the game. Just as the cells of our bodies change over time, so do the cells of business activities and outcomes. So even the responses to well-established research findings may have to be revisited and re-validated over time. It is therefore quite possible that different variables lead to varying evaluations of firms, with tracking them leading to bifurcated results based on different priorities. Take Apple as an example. The firm is admired by consumers worldwide for its consumer friendly products, its innovative ideas, its stylish approach, and its management as portrayed to the outside. In international marketing, Apple has achieved iconic status with its powerful brand. In 2011, when Apple Chairman Steve Jobs died, the firm became, according to the price of its shares, the most valuable publicly held company in the world.

In 2012, Millward Brown's BrandZ Top 100 Most Valuable Global Brands report ranked Apple the highest. Interbrand's Best Global Brands 2011 report ranked Apple in eighth place. Yet in spite of, or perhaps even because of, all these strengths and successes, Apple is being attacked for its production processes—particularly when it comes to its international sourcing. The company has been widely criticized for its treatment of workers in its Chinese production facilities, even though most of these facilities are owned by suppliers outside the company. The attacks against Apple can be labeled "relentless," and The New York Times reported in January 2012 that, "Problems are as varied as onerous work environments and serious——sometimes deadly—safety problems. Employees work excessive overtime, in some cases seven days a week, and live in crowded dorms. Some say they stand so long that their legs swell until they can hardly walk." Among the choir of such accusations, there have been a number of charges that turned out not to be true.

When confronted with the disparity between facts and claims of wrongful treatment, the accusers helpfully pointed out that it had been their intention all along to simply highlight what "probably is done wrong," not to deliver a catalog of actual shortcomings. Such public debates, delivered with widely differing ground rules, can result in the obfuscation—rather than the clarification—of actual conditions and the need for change. We will therefore, in the next issue of Marketing Management, develop a very specific focus on the relationship between Apple and its key independent supplier in China, named Foxconn. We will evaluate how this relationship with more than one-million Foxconn workers is managed and guided by Apple. We also will look at what steps might be needed so consumers not only enjoy the fine products they purchase from Apple, but can also feel at ease about the quality of work environment and social responsibility shaping the lives of workers.

Index

OTHER TITLES IN THE INTERNATIONAL BUSINESS COLLECTION

Tamer Cavusgil, Georgia State; Michael Czinkota, Georgetown; and Gary Knight, Willamette University, *Editors*

- *A Strategic and Tactical Approach to Global Business Ethics, Second Edition* by Lawrence A. Beer
- *Innovation in China: The Tail of the Dragon* by William H.A. Johnson
- *Dancing With The Dragon: Doing Business With China* by Mona Chung and Bruno Mascitelli
- *Making Sense of Iranian Society, Culture, and Business* by Hamid Yeganeh
- *Tracing the Roots of Globalization and Business Principles, Second Edition* by Lawrence A. Beer
- *Creative Solutions to Global Business Negotiations, Second Edition* by Claude Cellich and Subhash C. Jain

Announcing the Business Expert Press Digital Library

Concise e-books business students need for classroom and research

This book can also be purchased in an e-book collection by your library as

- *a one-time purchase,*
- *that is owned forever,*
- *allows for simultaneous readers,*
- *has no restrictions on printing, and*
- *can be downloaded as PDFs from within the library community.*
-

Our digital library collections are a great solution to beat the rising cost of textbooks. E-books can be loaded into their course management systems or onto student's e-book readers. The **Business Expert Press** digital libraries are very affordable, with no obligation to buy in future years. For more information, please visit **www.businessexpertpress.com/librarians**. To set up a trial in the United States, please email **sales@businessexpertpress.com**.

www.ingramcontent.com/pod-product-compliance
Lightning Source LLC
Chambersburg PA
CBHW071848200326
41519CB00016B/4289